D1106782

The Tangled Web

The Tangled Web

PHILIPPE GANIER-RAYMOND

Translated from the French by Len Ortzen

PANTHEON BOOKS   *A Division of Random House*

New York

Author's Note

I wish to express my sincere gratitude to the following, without whose help this book would not have been possible:

Beatrix Terwindt   Hubertus Gerardus Lauwers   Pieter Dourlein   Hermann Giskes   Joseph Schreieder   E. H. Cookridge   Eddie Chapman   Dr. L. de Jong, Director of the Netherlands State Institute for War Documentation   Major de Graaf

I have also consulted the report of the Netherlands Parliamentary Commission of Enquiry, the files of the newspaper *Het Parool*, and the following books:

Londres Appelle Pole Nord, by H. J. Giskes (Plon, Paris, 1958)   *Das War Das England Spiel*, by J. Schreider (Stutz Verlag, Munich, 1950)   *Inside North Pole*, by P. Dourlein (Kimber, London, 1953)   *Inside S.O.E.*, by E. H. Cookridge (Arthur Barker, London, 1967)

P. G-R.

Contents

Prologue

Lauwers wrapped himself in the thick blanket that Teller's wife had given him, then turned up the collar of his overcoat, so that only his numbed fingers and his face remained uncovered in the freezingly cold room. He opened the black case containing the transmitter-receiver, set it up, slipped the headphones over his aching ears and tried to make contact with London. But at first his numbed fingers would not obey him; the indicator quivered as though affected by the cold too. However, after a few minutes it steadied itself and at the same time an oscillating whistling filled the headphones. Then Hubertus Gerardus Lauwers – RLS to the British special services – began tapping out his call sign, forefinger and middle-finger glued to the little bakelite key.

He had always thought how marvellous it was to get in touch with London, and so quickly, with such a small apparatus, no more than a toy. And when London replied, sending him groups of morse at a regular rhythm, well spaced out (the English operator did not have to work in the atmosphere of anguish and suspense of Occupied Europe, so it was natural for his messages to be clearer and more even), then Lauwers was as amazed as if a miracle had taken place.

The door behind him suddenly opened and he felt a little of the cold wind sweeping the streets of The Hague as Teller came into the room. Lauwers knew practically nothing about him and his gentle, smiling, pretty wife, other than that they had something to do with the Dutch Resistance. A month previously, they had given him the use of this room in their apartment. Teller had offered to keep watch while Lauwers was transmitting, and the latter had accepted.

Teller, a tall, big man, was standing by the door, which he had closed behind him, and was silently watching Lauwers working the transmitter. Lauwers had a horror of this dumb presence behind him; it reminded him of an invigilator during a school examination. Without turning round or interrupting the sending of his code signal – 'The lamp is clean' – he asked, 'How are things outside?'

'Quiet,' said Teller. 'As usual . . .'

'Any detector-van?'

'I didn't notice one. Besides, they use private vans now. You can never tell. . . .'

'No soldiers about either?'

'There's some in a coach at the bottom of Farenheitsstraat. They're not armed. They're certainly there for some other reason.'

Lauwers suddenly stopped transmitting. With two sharp motions he closed the set and took off his headphones. Then he turned round to Teller and said almost spitefully: 'What makes you think that they're there for some other reason?'

'I don't know . . . they looked as if they're on leave. . . .'

Lauwers said no more, but began taking the set to pieces. Then, very carefully, he put each part back in the black case.

'You leaving?' said Teller.

'It's perhaps the best thing to do. . . . Yes.'

'In that case, leave the set here. My wife will find a good place to hide it.'

Lauwers hesitated a moment; but Teller was right, it would be stupid to risk being caught in the street with the radio-set. He stood up and looked round him; on the floor were the three pieces of paper with the three messages he had been going to send to London. He picked them up and stuffed them in his pocket.

It was just after seven in the evening of 6 March, 1942. Two men who had agreed to meet at the corner of Farenheitsstraat and Cyprusstraat, a little way from the centre of The Hague, arrived almost at the same time, each in a car and accompanied by several colleagues. The two were Major Hermann Giskes of the *Abwehr* (the German Army Intelligence Service) and *Kriminalrat* Joseph Schreieder. The former was in civilian clothes, the latter was wearing his Gestapo uniform. The *Abwehr* officers had come in an inconspicuous French car with Dutch number-plates, but Himmler's men had not thought discretion necessary and were in a big grey Mercedes with a German Army sign and a pennant on the offside front mudguard. The two cars parked one behind the other in Cyprusstraat. A strong wind was driving the snow forward, preventing it from settling on the windscreens and obscuring the view.

Hermann Giskes and Joseph Schreieder were probably wondering whether they were wasting their time, whether they had done right to believe Ridderhoff, the Dutch informer who, on their orders, had been feeding false information to the clandestine radio operator RLS for weeks past. Schreieder and Giskes had very different hierarchical superiors, but neither would have been forgiven for letting a low informer lead him up the path. However, Georges Ridderhoff had already given proof of his capabilities. Since December 1941, for 500 guilders a month – a very reasonable rate – *Abwehr* agent F2087 had penetrated the Resistance group commanded by Captain Van den Berg and had succeeded not only in locating a number of radio operators but had gained the confidence of the Resistance leaders to the extent of being asked, in February, to take charge of the reception of arms dropped by parachute!

It was almost too good to be true. How could Ridderhoff – F2087, a slovenly, vulgar creature – inspire anyone's confidence, Giskes wondered? Moreover, his past history as a smuggler of opium and diamonds was well known in Amsterdam and The Hague. Giskes could not understand how such a person had been able to make himself accepted by idealists, and this worried him. On the other hand, he knew from playing back messages picked up and recorded by detector vans that RLS had in fact sent to London all the 'information' – false troop movements, imaginary sailings of German naval units – which he himself had given to agent F2087. And when the latter had told him that the moment was ripe, that in one fell swoop he could destroy the network of British agents in Holland, he had decided to make the attempt.

At about twenty minutes past seven Giskes saw the unmistakable figure of his elderly second-in-command, Captain Wuhr, hurrying towards him, moleskin hat crammed over his ears, head buried in his muffler and both hands in his pockets. Giskes quickly lowered the car window. Wuhr, seen through a flurry of snow, was looking most cheerful.

'They're coming,' he said.

Lauwers and Teller were out in the street, walking fast; but they looked no different from the few other people hurrying homewards or seeking a café to get out of the wind and snow. Lauwers glanced back when they had gone about fifty yards, but no one was following them. A coachload of German soldiers was parked on the other side of the road. Teller had been right; they were obviously on short leave and about to go into a cabaret show. Lauwers breathed again. He almost thought of turning back and starting to transmit again. But it was too late now. London would be busy with messages from other agents in France and Yugoslavia. However, it was not very important, the information he had to send could easily wait till tomorrow; the arrival of the battlecruiser *Prinz Eugen* at Schiedam did not seem to him to have great strategic value. He and Teller had instinctively slowed their steps in their relief. They were still free, and began to laugh and joke as though wanting to convince one another of the fact. They raised their voices against the noise of the wind.

'I know a café lower down the street where they've still got some pre-war gin. Let's go there,' suggested Teller.

Lauwers agreed. They reached the corner of Cyprusstraat and were about to cross over when a grey Mercedes came into the kerb, splashing them, and a group of men in green and black sprang out of it. The two were at once overcome, searched for arms and made to stand against the wall. Meanwhile, another car had arrived and stopped in front of the Mercedes. Some men in grey overcoats tumbled from it, one of them holding a smallcalibre pistol. The *Abwehr* took over from the Gestapo and handcuffed Lauwers, while Schreieder's men dragged Teller into the Mercedes. Lauwers gave a cry as he saw the big man struggling ineffectually against the kicks and blows.

Lieutenant Teller was in fact just an officer but without any secrets – just an ordinary prey. He ended up in a concentration camp, where he met his death.

Lauwers was not knocked about, merely taken prisoner; nor was he insulted. The man holding him by the upper arm (it was Major Giskes) was not hurting him, and in other circumstances the hold might have passed for a friendly gesture or a sign of complicity. As he was led quickly to the other car Lauwers was thinking that he ought never to have lent his revolver. . . .

The car was driven up the street to where the Tellers lived. It all happened with great speed – and almost silently, probably because of the snow. Less than five minutes later, Lauwers found himself back in the room where he had been transmitting. Teller's wife was sitting on a chair, making an effort not to cry. She stared at Lauwers, unable to grasp what had happened. Probably because she was pregnant, they had not handcuffed her.

PART ONE *The Vice*

I

The Army in the Shadows

On the Continent, it was all over. First Poland had been overrun, then Denmark and Norway, Holland and Belgium, and now France had asked for an armistice. Guderian's Panzers had routed an out-of-date army on the same battlefields as those of the Franco-Prussian War of 1870. After the breakthrough at Sedan, the Germans had reached the Seine, then the Loire. The last of the BEF had re-embarked, and on 20 June 1940, Hitler told the *Reichstag*: 'England will soon be conquered. Mr Churchill must be thinking of seeking refuge in Canada.'

Hermann Goering, surrounded by his staff, was looking through his field-glasses at the cliffs of Dover, which were shrouded in mist. The Air Marshal was optimistic, even more optimistic than the *Führer*. He was convinced that the *Luftwaffe* alone could bring Britain to her knees in a few weeks. Hitler, however, was hesitant. As a gesture, which perhaps he thought might be accepted, he made a peace offer to Britain. Two days later, on 22 July, Lord Halifax informed the House of Commons that he had rejected it. There had never been any question of coming to terms with Nazi Germany. Even before the Battle of Britain had been won, while a handful of Hurricanes and Spitfires alone defended the free world, Prime Minister Winston Churchill was already thinking of taking the offensive.

Proof of his attitude is his minute to his Chief of Staff, General Ismay, on 6 June 1940: 'What arrangements are being made for good agents in Denmark, Norway, Belgium, Holland, and along the French coast?' Ismay was at a loss. Dunkirk had just fallen, the evacuation of the British Forces was hardly completed, and the French Government was about to withdraw to Bordeaux; the roads of France were filled with refugees, and the army was retreating in disorder after an unprecedented defeat. But Churchill did not waste time examining the causes of the disaster. Ismay received another note: 'I want operations to be carried out by specially trained men, capable of spreading terror ... the lives of German troops on the Continent must be made an intense torment ...' Churchill is said to have summed up his intention in one short, daring phrase, scrawled on the back of an old envelope – 'Set Europe ablaze!' He had decided to kindle a fire which would keep the war alight all over Occupied Europe; and fuel was added to it throughout the next four years.

The Special Operations Executive (SOE) came into being on 19 July 1940. The name of the organisation was deliberately vague for Churchill intended to keep it out of the hands of the War Office and the Intelligence chiefs. As one of his Ministers said: 'It's a question of turning out gangsters. And you'll never make gangsters out of officers.' Churchill knew this better than anyone. No regular officer or professional Intelligence agent would have been able to do what was asked of the volunteers who created SOE. They had to be newcomers, untainted and true, brave men who were not necessarily brutal but cold-blooded and full of nerve, almost superhuman. Obviously, they were bound to be amateurs, from all walks of life and from abroad.

They were reaching Britain in hundreds – Dutch, Norwegians, Belgians, and French. Many had gone aboard British vessels at Dunkirk or Ostend. Others had escaped in fishing-boats, and some young Frenchmen reached Dover in a canoe. The fact that they were determined to continue the fight was already a point in their favour. However, it was highly probable, even certain, that the Germans had slipped a few spies in amongst all these defeated soldiers escaping to England. But they would be sorted out later. The first priority was to set up an organisation able to carry out Churchill's plan to 'centralise all subversive and sabotage operations against the enemy', in other words to create a secret army in Nazi-occupied Europe.

Churchill put in charge of SOE the oddest bunch of people imaginable. Hugh Dalton, the Minister of Economic Warfare, was given the overall responsibility, and under him was a lifelong friend of the Prime Minister, Charles Hambro, a member of a family of City bankers. The director of training and operations was Colonel Colin Gubbins,[1] a shrewd man who was more politically than militarily inclined, but was an old hand at Intelligence work – which was most important. Below him were the amateurs: two colonels who had been prominent in the Scout movement, three journalists and a man who had been studying for the priesthood – each had an office at 82 Baker Street, previously the headquarters of Marks and Spencer. On the door to the building was a name-plate saying 'Inter-Service Research Bureau', which could have meant anything. The place had all the appearance of a private detective agency run by retired policemen, such as existed by the dozen in that part of London. In August 1940, SOE had successfully carried out its first mission – to set up unnoticed.

Not far from Baker Street – in the Marylebone Road, in Dorset Square, Wimpole Street – were other obscure offices with equally vague name-plates for various Sections of SOE, one for each of the German-occupied countries – the Polish Section, the Norwegian, Yugoslav, Danish, Belgian, French, and Dutch Sections. This last had at its head a Captain (later Colonel) De Bruyne.

The members, atmosphere and setting of SOE might have come straight out of a thriller by Agatha Christie; there was even a dilapidated country house, near the Welsh border. A selected group of Army Signallers had been sent there, to receive the messages from radio operators despatched to the continent and to send them orders from Baker Street. These Signallers had strict orders not to try to understand the meaning of the messages which passed through their hands, and they soon had that dull look of conscientious men who lack any real idea of the significance of the work entrusted to them. If the Germans had kidnapped one of them and tortured him, they would have learned nothing of the work of SOE.

By August 1940, the organisation was ready to function. It resembled many another British secret service—the Special Branch or the Intelligence Service—in that it consisted of a great number of tentacles linked to an invisible head. But the missions to be given to SOE agents were of a very different nature to those given to the special police or Intelligence agents. It all added up to preparing the way for the invasion of Europe! Even before the Dun-

[1] Later Major-General Sir Colin Gubbins.

kirk evacuation ended, Churchill had got naval engineers to make a model of a landing-craft to hold twenty-five soldiers and with bows that could be lowered like a drawbridge. Many craft of this kind were to be seen on the Normandy landing beaches in June 1944. SOE had its share of birth pangs and administrative difficulties. The War Office insisted on seeing all messages received from agents. The Intelligence Service refused to allow espionage – an old family business – to fall into the hands of foreigners. Consequently, the heads of Sections could not take any important decisions. Their job was solely to train agents and select those to be despatched. Not surprisingly, the exiled Allied leaders took a dim view of all this. Had not Churchill himself declared that all the Allied nations would fight side by side as equals? The Allied Governments in exile were calmed down. It was pointed out to them that operations on such a vast scale had to be centralised. Nevertheless, their leaders considered themselves snubbed, and after the war did not hesitate to speak of 'perfidious Albion'.

In Nazi-occupied Europe, 'blood and tears' flowed. Torture and death awaited the brave, determined SOE agents. It was hideous to think of them being sent in small groups to undermine and sabotage the huge, powerful German machine.

Never in history had Germany been so strong. Never had the Fatherland held down so many peoples. The men in the Baker Street offices were well aware of this, and that the German machine was working very efficiently. There was close collaboration between Himmler's Gestapo, Keitel's armies and Canaris's *Abwehr*. The time of discord and intrigue had not yet come : rats never leave ships which keep afloat.

In each occupied country the Nazis had set up a puppet government under a kind of proconsul appointed by Hitler, and Holland had come off worst of all in this respect. Arthur Seyss-Inquart was a thin-faced Austrian who wore rimless spectacles. He had betrayed his own country to Hitler and made no secret of his intention to bring about another *Anschluss* by making Holland a province of Germany. His chief weapon was a strong will, and powers of seduction that were out of the ordinary. He never took a direct part in any of the dirty work. Besides, the 'strong man' in Holland was not Seyss-Inquart but the colleague forced on him by Himmler – Hanns Albin Rauter, 'Reich Commissar for security matters', a real monster.

Rauter too was an Austrian, but otherwise the complete opposite of the cynical, stylish Viennese, Seyss-Inquart, who was so persuasive and a clever psychologist. Rauter was a machine, probably the most relentless, best-oiled machine ever produced by Himmler's organisation. It was not by accident that Holland had the highest percentage of people deported or shot in all Nazi-occupied countries, Poland excepted, by the time liberation came. Soon after arriving at The Hague, Rauter began wiping out everything which remotely resembled an organised Resistance movement. The Dutch Nazi Party was not spared, nor were the extremist organisations which had possibly considered collaborating with the Occupying Power at one time. Rauter wanted to reign supreme over Holland. His first step was to purge the country of Jews. Hundreds of them were put in cattle-trucks every week, on their way to Auschwitz or Treblinka. These trains always left on time. Rauter was a demon for punctuality, and these regular consignments to hellish torments were a matter of great pride to him – as is obvious from his periodical reports to Himmler, which were found after the war. They are nothing but a long, interminable and inhuman account in which deaths are reckoned by thousands. Rauter never held trials. He had been sent to Holland to suppress, so he suppressed. Many an evening, yellow posters with black borders were pasted up in The Hague, Amsterdam, Utrecht, informing the population that fifty hostages, sometimes more, had been shot at dawn. All for no real reason – because some exasperated Dutchman had struck a German soldier in the street, or because workers in Amsterdam had dared to go on strike.

It was terrible to think of a few agents trying to bring about a revolt in Holland – it would be like causing a riot in a concentration camp!

Major Giskes, whether in civilian clothes or in uniform, copied the stiff bearing of strutting Prussian officers of the Kaiser's time without looking too foolish. His sharp, shrewd eyes shone blue in a sparrow-like face which incongruously topped his burly body. A small moustache accentuated his thin mouth. At first glance, he seemed to be a hearty, jovial man, but when his small eyes lit up, there seemed to be nothing soft about him, and one became aware not only of his great intelligence but of a kind of hypnotic power. Hermann Giskes had great persuasive talents which enabled him to convince and make use of men for his own ends. These talents had delighted Admiral Canaris, and Giskes had become, if not his friend (for who could claim to be a friend of Canaris?) at least his favourite disciple.

Giskes, a northerner (born in Hamburg), was a lone wolf and a creature of Intelligence work. One wonders what would have become of him after the First World War if there had been no *Abwehr*. He joined the service in 1923, taking refuge in its secret ranks as the Weimar Republic was collapsing. He began to have ambitions, and gradually evolved his own technique of counter-espionage. During the 'thirties, while the Nazi Party was growing ever stronger, Giskes perfected his *Funkspiel* or 'radio-game'. In theory, the process was quite simple:

(*a*) A foreign agent sends his information back by radio. His hideout is discovered.

(*b*) An 'informer' is sent to get in touch with the agent, and then passes false information to him. The agent is taken in by this.

(*c*) The agent is arrested. He is told that, all unknowingly, he has been working for the *Abwehr* for months past. He is asked to continue to do so.

(*d*) The agent agrees, he is 'turned' or 'played back' – in other words, he transmits messages under German control. Or else he refuses, and then 'Justice takes its course'.

It was quite simple, but quite an art. You had to have a special ability to 'turn' an enemy agent, for not all of them are rogues. Threats were often not enough. It frequently happened that an agent preferred death to turning traitor. But Giskes had a genius for playing on the despair of his prisoners. As some of them said later: 'On seeing Giskes for the first time, you had the feeling of making a new friend.' He put over his charms in the grand manner, and in most cases the captured agents who had nothing more to lose agreed to work for him. And it is a remarkable fact, as has been proved, that Giskes never applied torture. 'I considered this procedure to be useless and degrading ... worthy only of Hitler's riff-raff (*Lumpengesindel*),' he has written.

It had its importance – that Giskes, like many upper-class Germans from the north, should have felt nothing but hatred and repulsion for the Nazis. The Alsatians with a shady past whom French Intelligence sent to report on German Navy movements at Bremen, Lubeck and Hamburg, and whom Giskes caught and turned, have testified that he never handed them over to the Gestapo for interrogation.

The war, however, obliged Giskes to work for the greater glory of the Nazis. In June 1940, the *Abwehr* sent him to Paris, where he had his office at the Hotel Lutétia. He did not expect his stay in the French capital to last very long. His counter-espionage branch (111 C/2) reported direct to Army Command; neither the Gestapo nor the SS had the right to interfere in his affairs. Giskes embarked on a few 'dirty little tricks', as his friend, Field Marshal von Rundstedt, referred to that finesse of counter-espionage, the *Funkspiel*. Von Rundstedt knew nothing about Intelligence work (as became evident at the time of the Normandy landings!), but he was aware of the fact and left Giskes in peace. Giskes succeeded in turning two radio operators working in Paris for British Intelligence and in 'playing back' their radio sets. For a week, London accepted as genuine the false information which Giskes supplied to the captured agents. A whole week! It was a record. 'The British stopped *playing with us* when they noticed that something was missing from or had been inserted in the code being used,' Giskes told me after the war.

In addition to his codes, every radio operator working for the British was given a 'security check'. This was a deliberate spelling mistake or a key-sentence which must come up in the clear when the message was deciphered in London. These individual security checks were supposed to be the agent's way of showing he was still at liberty. Every radio operator was told before leaving England that if his check failed to appear in any message he would be deemed to have been captured and be working under German control.

The great weakness in Giskes's method was that he did not know whether the turned agent had given him a false security check or not. But this mattered very little at the time, in 1940. Intelligence work had its importance, certainly, but was not vital at that stage in the war. It was only a 'branch' of the armies in the field. In 1940 Giskes's work was more like a party game played by well-bred opponents than real secret warfare.

'I knew through trustworthy sources that my opposite numbers respected me as much as I respected them. We were having a private war between men of similar breed, who hated the butchery of the battlefields.'

However, Hitler was about to attack Russia. Churchill had succeeded in raising an army in the shadows. Henceforth, espionage and counter-espionage would not have quite the same significance; instead of a game between well-bred opponents it was to be a fight without mercy.

On 22 June 1941, Hitler launched his divisions across the Russian plains. Von Rundstedt had been given command of Army Group South, and Major Giskes was expecting to join him. But Canaris was keeping an eye on things. Probably he had no wish for his protégé to hunt down Ukranian partisans. It may well be that he had less dirty work in view for Giskes. In any case, the major was posted to The Hague in August 1941.

Giskes was deep in thought while being driven north from Paris. He knew that in Holland he would not have the freedom of action he had enjoyed under Von Rundstedt. He knew that Rauter kept a tight hold on all branches of the German services, and he had always reacted badly to supervision. But his chief fear was that he would be obliged to dishonour himself by collaborating with the SS, the SD (*Sicherheitsdienst*), the SIPO (*Sicherheitspolizei*), and other police and security forces that came under Heinrich Himmler. Giskes wondered what he would do if told to take a part in the indiscriminate repressive measures ordered by the *Reichskommissar*. Giskes always looked at problems coolly, but this was a moral problem. He knew he was no saint, but nevertheless there were some things he refused to have anything to do with.

It was a dark night and pouring with rain when the car reached the frontier post. Through the water streaming down the car windows, Giskes could just see a few Dutch police in flapping waterproofs and two or three German *Feldgendarmes* in hooded greatcoats. The latter took his identity papers and examined them at length, passing them from one to the other before handing them back, soaking wet, to Giskes's driver. Then, with a brief gesture, Major Giskes was allowed to enter *Reichskommissar* Rauter's domain.

The German Army counter-espionage service in Holland

(*Abwehr* 111/F) had requisitioned a building in the seaside resort of Scheveningen on the outskirts of The Hague. It was nothing like as comfortable as the four-star Hotel Lutétia in Paris. The Germans took the war seriously in Holland, and the secret services kept themselves secret. It was a secluded, grey stone building dating from the end of the nineteenth century, and was surrounded by barbed wire. Visitors were admitted through an underground passage at the back. Giskes was not displeased by all this. He liked to work in isolated surroundings, and he thought that the wooded grounds and barbed-wire would protect him from visits by Gestapo chiefs as much as from terrorist attacks. He soon named the place 'the Citadel'.

However, when he had seen his office staff, Giskes felt less satisfied. He had hoped to have a few enthusiastic young officers under his orders, or a few wiley professionals of his own kind, but he found a tight little world of timorous men more concerned to avoid being sent to the Russian front than to go hunting for enemy agents. Giskes also found that his immediate superior, known as Colonel Hofwald, was scared stiff – not of going to Russia, but of the Gestapo. He had made no protest when Rauter had decided to deal with counter-espionage matters himself and in his own way: arrests, interrogations, trials (optional), executions. The *Abwehr* activities were confined to a few minor, routine affairs; it located enemy agents and made out reports which were forwarded to higher echelons. Giskes was aghast at discovering that, by its docile attitude, the *Abwehr* at The Hague had become closely associated with Himmler's SD and Gestapo. However, it was no less than he had expected.

When Giskes reported to Colonel Hofwald he realised that this plump man who was offering him a Dutch cigar was not too happy at seeing him. The interview did not last very long. Hofwald was obviously wondering what had led Canaris to send him this eager officer, this specialist in active counter-espionage. One had only to look at the major to realise that he had no intention of dozing behind his new office desk.

'May I have permission, sir,' said Giskes, 'to make some changes among my staff? I should like to bring up one or two of the men from Paris who are used to working with me.'

'Do whatever you wish, Major,' Hofwald replied with a sigh.

'But in heaven's name, don't get *me* on the wrong side of the Gestapo. . . .'

Giskes gave a little smile, saluted, slightly clicked his heels and went out. Everything considered, the colonel's slackness was going to be useful to him.

Later that day, walking along a corridor in the Citadel, he met an officer he had known in the First World War, Captain Richard Wuhr. Giskes was glad to find that he had one man among his staff on whom he could rely.

'How are you?' Wuhr greeted him in a strong Swabian accent, thrusting out a great hairy hand. He was now a wheezy, red-faced, sly-looking, elderly man. 'It's a long time since we last saw each other,' he said as one old friend to another.

He had omitted to salute, and besides, Giskes disliked such a jovial approach in public, especially when the whole unit needed shaking up. Giskes at once put Wuhr in his place. 'Stand easy, Captain,' he said stiffly. 'I'm glad to have you with me.'

Wuhr realised that the office was in for a number of changes.

'I shall be relying on you a great deal, Wuhr,' the major continued. 'First of all, I want you to make me out a report on the activities of British agents in Holland. Then we'll see what action to take. That's all for now. Carry on.'

Giskes found the report on his desk the following morning.

'As I read it, I realised that the enemy had a different aspect now, that we no longer had to deal with just a few isolated agents despatched to Europe by the Intelligence Service. It was clear that a whole organisation with powerful means at its disposal was beginning to operate in Holland. Two questions sprang to mind: First, what was this organisation? Second, for the British, who were still on the defensive, to send men and arms to Holland could only mean that they regarded Holland as having great strategic importance. What, then, were the British planning?'[1]

Giskes, sitting alone at his desk, had guessed the existence of SOE and was close to deducing what Churchill had in mind for the future – the invasion of Europe.

On 14 May 1940, at Rotterdam, Crown Princess Juliana and Prince Bernhard went aboard a British destroyer to sail to England. One of the Dutch guard-of-honour drawn up on the

[1] Giskes, H. J., *Spione Uberspielen Spione*, Hamburg, 1951.

quayside was Private Van Dam. He was in despair. Rotterdam was ablaze, German troops were only a few miles away and there were few Dutch forces still capable of resistance. Private Van Dam suddenly felt completely abandoned. Several witnesses have told how, when the heiress to the Dutch throne, her husband and children had gone on board the destroyer, Van Dam – a giant of a man who broke everything he touched – threw his rifle to the ground and then, not content with that, picked it up again and broke it across his knee. No action was taken against him. Two months later, Van Dam reached England via France and Spain, and joined the Dutch Forces. He was killed fighting the Japanese.

Pieter Dourlein was also on the quayside at Rotterdam that day, with other survivors from the cruiser *Jan van Galen* which had just been dive-bombed in the port and was sinking fast. Pieter Dourlein was a tough young sailor but was crying openly. There must be some way of getting revenge on the criminals in field-green uniform who had sunk his fine ship and were destroying his homeland. . . .

Dourlein joined the Resistance, then twice almost lost his life trying to reach England. Eventually, in June 1941, he and a friend stole a motor launch and headed out to sea. The engine broke down and they had to row until, half dead from thirst, they were picked up by the destroyer *Wardour*, whose captain told them they had been drifting into a minefield. Three days later, Dourlein was in London and was taken to see Prince Bernhard. The latter, after hearing his story, told him to start learning English, as men like him were needed for 'work out of the ordinary'.

Hundreds of Dutchmen of Dourlein's stamp were reaching England, not all from the continent. Some came from the Dutch East Indies, like Hubertus Gerardus Lauwers, a journalist who had left his tropical paradise to join the fight for freedom in Europe. All were sent on arrival to the Patriotic School in London, for security clearance, and were closely interrogated for several days. Pieter Dourlein saw it was not altogether pointless when he was present at the arrest of a young 'Frenchman' who was carrying a complete 'spy kit' – another German agent caught!

Such happenings were rare, however. And the Dutch arrivals, people like Baatsen, a singer, Jambroes, a professor, Kloos, Boogaart and Arenose, were untarnished, the pure-in-heart, of whom a British officer said later: 'Only someone mad, unthinking or extremely simple would have agreed to go on the missions given to them.' In fact SOE, the 'work out of the ordinary', called for men who had never really grown up, and nearly all the Dutch who volunteered for it were under thirty.

One morning in December 1940, a dark-haired young man of average height, though with slightly bent shoulders, arrived at the Patriotic School. He gave his name as Van der Reyden. 'I used to be a member of the Dutch Nazi Party,' he frankly told the interrogating officer. 'But I was too young then to know what I was doing, and I've regretted it ever since. I want to go and fight the barbarians who've invaded my homeland.'

He spoke clearly and without much emotion. The officer looked steadily at him; he seemed sincere. For several hours, Van der Reyden was questioned about his past life, his family, and the friends he still had in Holland. He answered quite freely, revealing a somewhat limited intelligence and a certain absence of scruples, but also a firm desire to be revenged 'on all those Fascists who took me in'. A solid young man with spirit. Several other officers and even a psychiatrist took over the interrogation, and they all concluded that Van der Reyden was totally incapable of duplicity. The following morning they were all agreed that he should be allowed to train as a special agent.

2

The Cell

Hubertus Lauwers woke up in a small room that was amazingly clean for a prison cell. The glossy cream paint on the walls was unsullied by any scrawl. The bed was a real bed, not just a drop-bench. A powerful yellow light was shining from the ceiling. Lauwers had got over his fears. All his anxiety – of being caught, of talking – was in the past. He had been caught and he had not talked. His finger-nails, his teeth and his jaw were still intact; he had not been tortured, or even manhandled.

Major Giskes was just what Lauwers had always imagined an *Abewhr* officer to be like—plenty of swagger, calm, with the persuasive looks of a Germanic Janus. Lauwers was not surprised that such a man had not ill-treated him. But he could expect to be subjected to torture tomorrow or in the very near future. Giskes had tried to win him over, but without success. Lauwers was not the kind of man to be 'turned' by gentle treatment, kid-glove methods, with a smile and the offer of a cigarette. So, naturally, the harsh treatment would come next, and soon. Lauwers – a cool head on a weak body – was not afraid, for he possessed a very effective secret weapon; he could lose consciousness almost at will.

Lauwers was feeling rather proud of himself. When, a year previously, he had jumped into the night, his pockets filled with lead (his slim build was not sufficient weight for the parachute to open automatically), he had not considered himself an important person. He knew he had a difficult mission, and that months of training had gone into making him a good amateur radio operator, but he was far from thinking that his actions could have a decisive effect on the course of the war. Yet Giskes had not only treated him as a human being, once the two were alone together in the major's office, but had also shown him some respect. Lauwers could not help thinking that he was no ordinary prisoner. When the major had discovered his rank, he had made a point of always addressing him as 'Lieutenant Lauwers'. It was odd, he thought, that he had had to wait to be captured before being given the respect due to an officer. Of course, that was all part of Giskes's method, or more precisely the preliminaries to it. But Lauwers was thinking of the British and Dutch officers, and especially of the NCOs, who had trained him and his comrades at Ringway, near Manchester (parachute jumping), at Reading (radio) and at Haslemere (Commando course). For months, they had been subjected to insults and rough treatment, told they were a worthless lot and not fit for the job. Lauwers knew it was all simulated, to prepare them for facing the real thing. But it had distressed him, and he smiled now at the thought that the enemy had so far treated him with humanity.

There was no window or skylight to the cell, so Lauwers did not know if it was day or night. But to judge by the silence in the corridor, the *Abwehr* men had not yet started their day's work. He thought it might be about six in the morning, and he laid down again and closed his eyes; but he could not get to sleep, the light was too strong. Giskes had given orders for it to be left on – a man who is kept awake breaks down all the sooner.

Lauwers did not have long to wait. A quarter of an hour later there came the tramp of heavy boots and harsh cries echoed along the corridor. A key rattled in the lock, the door swung open and a corporal entered carrying a can of hot coffee. He poured some out for Lauwers, who drank it (real coffee, with sugar!) telling himself that it probably contained some special drug. The corporal offered him some more and Lauwers accepted it. Then Major Giskes came in and the corporal left.

Giskes was wearing a grey, double-breasted suit of English cut and material, Lauwers noticed. He had instinctively stood up as the major entered, and immediately regretted this mark of subordination.

'Be seated, Lieutenant Lauwers.'

There was no chair in the cell, so Giskes sat on the bed by the other's side. He drew a brown tortoise-shell cigarette case from his pocket and held it out to Lauwers.

'You have refused to reveal your code, Lieutenant Lauwers, and I consider that to be quite legitimate. I now repeat to you what I said yesterday. While I respect you as a soldier, as an officer, I've nothing but contempt for those who sent you here. Those people have made you believe you were fighting for your country, but you're not! They sent you here to stir up civil war. The British would like to see you distributing arms to irresponsible men, they would like to see your country torn by bloody strife! Do you follow me? But, personally, I want none of this fratricidal war, none of such a bloody business.'

Giskes continued speaking in the same distinct tones, clearly enunciating every word.

'Our interests are the same. A stop must be put to this lunacy before it is too late. Otherwise more men of your kind, brave men, will be parachuted into Holland and captured by my units. It will then become impossible for me to save them from the firing-squad.'

Giskes was putting over a telling argument. He had seen at once that Lauwers was a sentimentalist and that the thought of his colleagues being killed would weigh heavily upon him. Giskes made another point, like someone driving a wedge into a young tree that was beginning to totter.

'Besides, don't think you are the first SOE agent that we've captured.'

For the first time, Giskes let fall the name of the organisation which had despatched Lauwers to Holland, and the German saw his prisoner give a start. It was the right method to employ – to shake Lauwers, to startle him while talking in a relaxed manner. And so, in the early morning of 7 March 1942, the *Abwehr* major began telling Lauwers about his counter-espionage activities since being posted to The Hague.

Major Giskes would probably have remained in his burrow, powerless inside the Citadel, like his superior officer, Colonel Hofwald, if a small, almost bald man with a heavy round head, wearing a tight-fitting SS uniform, had not entered his office on the morning of 3 September 1941. This man was a former *Kriminalrat* (equivalent to Detective Superintendent), Joseph Schreieder, whom Himmler had made an SS *Sturmbannführer*, a rank equivalent to that of Lieutenant-Colonel.

A week previously, the Gestapo had caught a young Dutchman named Hans Zomer. On him were found lists of signal codes and names and addresses of Dutch Resistance leaders. Zomer refused to talk, even under torture. Rauter had demanded that he be executed, and this was done. Schreieder, although not being directly concerned with the case (he was head of the Gestapo at The Hague, and Zomer had been arrested in Rotterdam), nevertheless felt that a better method could be employed to succeed in the fight against enemy agents and terrorists. He was probably the first Gestapo chief to see the need of close collaboration with the *Abwehr* specialists.

When Schreieder first entered Giskes's office, the aristocratic *Abwehr* major gave a shudder of distaste. The podgy Bavarian policeman was perspiring freely, and Giskes (two baths a day and a shower after lunch) was distressed by such lack of personal hygiene. Schreieder kept fluttering his flabby, well-manicured hands, and continually addressed Giskes as *Lieber Kamerad*, although this was the first time they had met. In addition, there was the uniform with the SS badges, a silent menace which would have weighed heavily on anyone.

However, Giskes was curious to know what had brought Schreieder to his office. The Gestapo chief took some time to get to the point.

'*Lieber Kamerad* Giskes,' he began, 'the Zomer affair has been dealt with in a deplorable manner. I'm entirely in agreement with you about it.' (Giskes had not uttered a word about the Zomer affair.) 'But you know as well as I do that we can't always do as we should like.' (He pointed to the ceiling.) 'I expect that you, dear comrade Giskes, have your hands tied too. Briefly, in your interests as well as mine, this is what I propose. . . .'

Major Giskes disliked any stranger, especially one of Himmler's men, being anxious about his '*interests*'. But he made a great effort to hide his irritation, contenting himself with tapping on his desk with one finger. What the *Kriminalrat* had to propose was truly astounding.

'From now on,' he continued in his Bavarian accent, 'we ought to combine our efforts. Your methods, and your experience, coupled with our very extensive means. . . .'

He had ended on a note of interrogation. Would Giskes agree to combine their efforts for the greater benefit of German counter-espionage in Holland? Giskes was careful not to show too much enthusiasm. He replied, a little curtly, that he was not opposed to their offices collaborating, provided the Gestapo did not try to put its nose into the private affairs of the *Abwehr*.

'In your interests as well as mine,' said Giskes with a smile, 'it is important that each stays in his respective position.'

Schreieder agreed, and Giskes shook his hand. The major later wrote in his memoirs that he had listened without pleasure to Schreieder's proposals. The fact remains that the Gestapo chief's initiative was to enable the *Abwehr* major to carry out operations on a par with his capabilities. With the support of the Gestapo, Giskes and his staff were to show the true worth of German counter-espionage.

On the following day, Giskes learned that it was Colonel Hofwald, his slack, scared chief, who had persuaded Schreieder to go and see him. But the suggestion had come in the first place from Admiral Canaris in Berlin.

Giskes, sitting on the army bed next to Lauwers, did not go into all the details of the meeting with Schreieder. That did not concern his prisoner and in any case would not help to turn him. Giskes's aim at this stage was to impress upon Lauwers the fact that he was caught in a fine mesh, that the smooth-running partnership of the *Abwehr* and the Gestapo represented immense power. Not a single agent sent by the British could possibly escape them. Lauwers said nothing; during his training in England he had been put on his guard against such blandishments. He merely shrugged his shoulders now and again. He was really not interested in what Giskes was telling him. His mind was running on something else, something which had nothing to do with SOE, the *Abwehr*, nor even the war. He kept wondering who could possibly have betrayed them.

Giskes felt sure of it, that Lauwer's weak point was his blind confidence in the British organisation, in its efficiency. By chipping away at that, Giskes hoped to shake Lauwer's confidence and eventually break him down. So Giskes changed his tone and related the events leading to the capture of Lauwers and Teller. . .

On the night of 20 November 1941, a British motor-launch had landed agent Willem Jacobas Van der Reyden on the beach at Scheveningen. It had been a simple matter. At that period in the war, two years before the construction of the Atlantic Wall, the coast was very weakly guarded. But why Van der Reyden? It is a mystery why this ex-Dutch Nazi was chosen to be one of the first to 'set Europe ablaze'. His mission was to link up with another agent, Ter Laak, who was dropped by parachute two days later, and make contact with Resistance groups, organise them and train them in subversive warfare. A wide enough directive! Actually, London was hoping for a report from the two agents as to the possibilities of organising an active Resistance in Holland.

Van der Reyden and Ter Laak wandered about for some weeks, from The Hague to Rotterdam, Apeldoorn to Breda. They knocked at the door of a 'friend' in the evening and left the following morning. Every three days, Van der Reyden set up his transmitter and sent a report to London, and each time it was to say they had still not discovered a Resistance group. They were taking enormous risks by contacting people posing as Resistance men, and on 13 February 1942, the inevitable happened. Schreieder, who had known about them for some time, had them arrested in the street in Rotterdam.

Schreieder, who was not without vanity, possibly wanted to show Giskes that he could beat the *Abwehr* at its own game. In any case, he decided to have Van der Reyden interrogated and turned by his Gestapo men. They were most surprised when the agent readily talked. There was no need even to threaten him. He revealed everything, his code and all he knew about the Special Operations Executive, the names of its officers including the head of the Dutch Section, Colonel De Bruyne, and the location of the training schools and camps. Information gushed from him, and he went on to give details of the Baker Street offices and the number of staff employed. He said that a massive plan was in preparation, and that within a year the German armed forces in Europe would be constantly harassed by armies from the shadows.

Van der Reyden revealed all this as calmly as though sitting in a drawing-room; the handcuffs on him seemed quite out of place. The Gestapo men listening to him were taking notes as if hearing a report from one of their own informers. Van der Reyden spoke clearly and firmly, and his face shone with sincerity. He convinced the Germans as he had the interrogating officers at the Patriotic School. Besides, the information he gave coincided so well with what the Germans already knew that there was no reason for them not to believe him.

It was three hours before Van der Reyden finally stopped talking. He had told everything! Then came the Germans' turn.

'I suppose,' said *Kriminalrat* Joseph Schreieder, 'that you know the fate of spies captured in wartime?'

Van der Reyden admitted that he did know.

'There's one way for you to avoid it,' Schreieder continued. 'A very simple way – just agree to work for us.'

The Dutchman said that he was quite prepared to transmit to London under German control, that anything was better than facing a firing-squad.

'Good,' said Schreieder. 'Then we'll make a start tomorrow.' Van der Reyden was taken to the cell next door, a real prison cell with iron bars and smelling of sweat and urine. He stretched out on the bench and fell asleep almost at once.

He was woken up at dawn. Schreieder had given orders for him to be handcuffed. Apparently nothing had caused him to change his mind during the night; he still seemed quite calm and prepared to cooperate with the Germans.

'If I'm not mistaken,' Schreieder said to him, 'your scheduled time to transmit is eight-thirty?'

'Quite true.'

'We've no time to waste. Come along.'

But Van der Reyden asked for some coffee and to be allowed to shave. (He gave the impression of being some clerk about to leave for the office.) Schreieder had a bowl of hot dish-water brought to him and sent out for a barber.

At eight o'clock he was hustled into a black car and put in the back seat between two uniformed policemen. They were so broad that Van der Reyden could see little of the gaping buildings of the devastated city as they drove through it. Some way out of Rotterdam, the car drew up at a small house. There was a sentry on the door, and a very tall aerial was fixed to the roof. Van der Reyden was taken inside and found himself in a typical Dutch sitting-room with a bust on the mantelpiece and family photos smiling from the yellowish walls. On an oval table covered with a cloth was a radio transmitter that he recognised as his; it was plugged in and tuned to the London reception station. Schreieder gave him a sheet of paper bearing fanciful 'secret' messages.

'Now get to work,' said the *Kriminalrat*.

Van der Reyden heard the three Germans behind him draw

in their breath, like spectators at a circus when the trapeze artists are ready on their little platforms high above the ring. The Dutchman was an excellent radio operator, and in a few minutes he was in contact with London. His touch on the Morse key was sharp and at an even rhythm, neither too slow nor too fast. Unlike many amateur radio operators, he did not increase speed at the end of a group of letters, and if he thought he had made a mistake he began again. One of the three men behind him fully appreciated his skill – Lieutenant Heinrichs, who was in charge of the radio detection and interception service of the Gestapo. He was keeping a close check on what the prisoner was transmitting.

It lasted less than fifteen minutes. London replied that reception had been very good and told Van der Reyden to make contact at the same time the following morning.

'I expect you're satisfied now,' said Van der Reyden, taking off his headphones and turning round to Schreieder.

'Entirely. It went off very well. We'll have another session tomorrow morning.'

It was then that Van der Reyden mustered some secret inner strength and looked the *Kriminalrat* straight in the eyes. 'Tomorrow,' he said, 'London won't reply. Nor the day after ... London won't ever reply.'

Schreieder's small eyes opened wide. 'What do you mean? Lieutenant Heinrichs! What does he mean?'

Lieutenant Heinrichs stammered a little as he said that Van der Reyden had kept to the messages given to him and had transmitted the coded text correctly.

'That's exactly why London now knows that I've been captured and was working under your control. I didn't make the deliberate mistake I ought to have done – my security check was missing.' And Van der Reyden burst out laughing.

One of the men darted forward to hit him, but Schreieder caught his arm.

'What did you take me for – a traitor?' said the Dutchman, still laughing.

Schreieder handed Van der Reyden over to other specialists (he himself could not stand the sight of a man being tortured), but the Dutchman never revealed his security check.

Nevertheless, despite this setback and having made himself look ridiculous, Schreieder had learned a number of things. More-

36

over, Van der Reyden's notebook contained names and addresses of Resistance men and details of many dropping-grounds.

Schreieder went to see Giskes, taking this newly-acquired information as a dowry for their marriage of convenience. The major knew how the Van der Reyden case had been dealt with, but he said nothing about it to Schreieder.

'This is excellent,' he said to the effusive Gestapo chief (Giskes could never get used to Bavarian glibness). 'What you've brought me is most interesting.'

Giskes became almost cordial, though still keeping his distance. 'Thanks to you, now we know what we're up against. Dispositions must be made to defeat the efforts of the organisation on the other side. And, if you agree, we'll share the work.'

Giskes put his big fist on the file that Schreieder had brought him. In a civil manner, but one which left no room for argument, he assumed command of the undertaking. And to let the *Kriminalrat* know that he was fully aware of the Gestapo's clumsy antics Giskes added: 'And, if you agree, we'll start acting intelligently. . . .'

Giskes had been talking to Lauwers for over an hour, sometimes in German, sometimes in Dutch – a schoolboy Dutch but correct enough, smacking of the 'Assimil' method of learning. He went on and on about agents who had been 'inevitably' caught before Lauwers and who had agreed (which was not true) to transmit to London under German control. But Lauwers had long since stopped listening to him. One thought was running through Lauwers's mind – what had happened to Thijs, his fellow agent who had been dropped with him to work as liaison officer with the Dutch Resistance? Thijs Takonis was a tall, dark-haired man with a swarthy complexion who hailed, like Lauwers, from the Dutch East Indies. He was often taken for a half-caste, but was probably descended from a Spanish family which had settled in the Netherlands at the time of the Habsburgs. Takonis spoke very little and never confided in anyone, noticed everything and forgot nothing. If it had not been for his distinctive appearance, he would have had all that was required to make a brilliant agent. He never slept in the same bed on two successive nights; he contacted Resistance groups and then disappeared again. However, Lauwers was thinking that whoever had informed about him must have known of his habits, and that Thijs met him three times a week to pass on the information gathered from Resistance groups. It was possible that Takonis had been caught by the Germans, that he had betrayed Lauwers.... No, that was crazy thinking! Lauwers had known Takonis for ten years (there was a photo of him at some party in the old suitcase that Lauwers had left in London). Takonis was staunch, a tough nut, probably the one man he could be sure would not talk.

Giskes was still purring away. He seemed to be in no hurry to get to the moment of Lauwers's capture, in spite of what he had said. He was very likely waiting for Lauwers to ask him questions. But the Dutchman remained silent; in an effort to dismiss the grim thoughts about Takonis, he was concentrating his mind on small but precise details – that he was dirty, that his shirt which had been clean two days ago was now sticking to his neck, that he needed a shave and would have liked to brush his teeth.... He had smoked all of Giskes's cigarettes and felt at a loss. He decided to speak.

'I don't see the connection between what you've been telling me and my arrest.'

He did not say 'our' arrest. He had forgotten about Teller.

'I'm coming to that,' said Giskes.

Then he told Lauwers how his colleague Captain Wuhr and Sergeant Willy Kupp had met Ridderhoff, the fat, bloated ex-smuggler, who said he was 'well in with some English spies'. This was in January 1942. Wuhr and Kupp had returned very elated and sent in a report to Giskes, who said it was fantastic but told them to keep in touch with the man. Later, Ridderhoff proved his worth. But Giskes did not believe it – or pretended not to. 'Go to the North Pole with your stories!' he told Wuhr and Kupp. They had persevered with Ridderhoff, however, and the traitor had earned his pay by telling them he was in the confidence of a 'half-caste from Arnhem', a British agent who could easily be fed false information.

Lauwers did not give a start at this point in Giskes's story, but he went red, and the other noticed it.

'You know this man, of course – "long Thijs"?'

'No, I don't. I don't know anyone called Thijs,' said Lauwers.

Giskes continued. Thijs, fed by Ridderhoff, whom he believed to be a patriot, had supplied Lauwers with false information. This had gone on for six weeks. Then the time had come (nearly all the members of Van den Berg's group were known to the *Abwehr* and Gestapo by then) to bring the game to an end.

'You didn't know it, Lieutenant Lauwers, but for three months you've been our go-between with London.'

Lauwers gave a shout. 'It's not true!' There was some pretence on his part, for he had no reason to doubt what Giskes had just told him. 'You're lying! You're just a dirty Boche!'

Giskes frowned at him. 'Lieutenant Lauwers, mind what you're saying. I've been perfectly polite with you. I advise you to be the same. In your own interest. Do you understand me?'

Lauwers nodded. He was not submitting, but he needed time to muster his strength again. His head was going round, his mind was in a fever. He was going to die – tomorrow or the next day, what did it matter – he would be taken out and shot, he had nothing more to lose. But he was not yet rebelling against his fate. Not everything Giskes had told him could be right. Undoubtedly the major had mixed the true and the false, to see how he would react. As he looked at Giskes, however, his face was clear enough, though drawn with fatigue.

'I don't know any of the men you've mentioned,' he murmured. 'I don't know who "long Thijs" is. I've never met anyone called Van der Reyden (this was true). I can't see what you're driving at.'

Giskes got no pleasure from this game. He mentally noted, as he had often done before, that the behaviour of captured agents was always the same. They became malleable not by suddenly breaking down but by giving in gradually. Lauwers was at the stage where an agent denied everything, disputed all along the line. But now that he had started replying to Giskes, he was on the downward slope. . . .

'As you refuse to believe that we know all about you,' said the major, 'I'll make a bargain with you. I'll bet you that our specialist can decode the first message you were going to send yesterday in less than five minutes. If he succeeds, then I shall expect you to tell us your code.'

'He can't succeed,' said Lauwers.

'Do you agree to my bargain? If you think we can't succeed, you've nothing to fear. On the other hand, if we do manage to decode your message, then it shouldn't be difficult for us to discover your code. It'll take a little longer, that's all. And, in the meantime, other soldiers like you will come floating down and fall into our hands. But they won't all be sent to me. A number of them will be interrogated by the Gestapo. And there's no need for me to tell you that the Gestapo treats its prisoners differently from us.'

Giskes had sharpened his tone. There was an edge to his voice indicating that Lauwers had to make up his mind quickly, that the major's patience would not last for ever.

'Lieutenant Lauwers, the fate of your comrades is in your hands,' he ended. 'You must help me to prevent this slaughter. Think the matter over.'

He stood up, told Lauwers that he would come for his reply the next morning, and left the cell. The door did not quite close behind him. For a minute or so, Lauwers could see into the grey, drab corridor and hear the various noises that came floating down it. Then, suddenly, he heard heavy footsteps and the shuffling sound of someone being dragged along. A draught or the jailer's hand made the cell door open wider. Lauwers saw two field-green soldiers pass by, grasping the arms of a tall, dark-haired man, stiff as a poker in clothes too big for him. He had not been beaten up; at least, there were no signs of violence on his face or hands. Then the cell door was slammed shut, and Lauwers was left alone with his thoughts.

He had just seen Takonis being led past.

3

Caught in the Mesh

Lauwers drew himself up. He was only twenty-five, and psychological preparation for his task had had no place in his training. He wondered what Giskes was getting at. The major held all the cards – power, and the means of breaking a code (at least, so he claimed). But he did not know, and never would know, Lauwers's security check. With any luck, he might not even suspect the existence of security checks. Lauwers still had the master card.

Soon after Giskes had left the cell, Lauwers was taken to the Binnenhoff, which had been the seat of the Dutch Parliament before the Gestapo took it over. Three black-clad Gestapo men took turns at interrogating him, but Lauwers was well aware that his fate would not be decided there. His case was not a straightforward police matter. He was being interrogated for the record, because German officialdom – like all others – wanted lots of cards in its files. The questions had no real importance. He was asked his peacetime job (journalist), whether he was married (no), where exactly he had been parachuted (he lied about this, just for devilment, saying that he had been put ashore at Kootwijk by a Royal Navy launch). The man in charge of the interrogation, a Sergeant May, seemed to be specially interested in how he had spent his time in England. Where did he go when on leave? And who with? Lauwers made it up. He named London cinemas he had never been in, and spoke of a girl, Doreen, who had never existed. This amused him a little and kept him alert. Oddly enough, the Gestapo was giving him a respite before again facing the more formidable arguments of Major Giskes. But Sergeant May suddenly and quite unexpectedly banged the table. The other two had drawn back slightly. He shone the desk lamp in Lauwers's face, just as in films.

'And now, Mister Lauwers, you're going to give me your code!'

It was the old trick, the startling change of tone, used by police everywhere. Lauwers should have been expecting it. He assumed a calm, collected voice before replying.

'I've already told Major Giskes – there is no question of revealing my code.'

Schreieder had given orders that Lauwers was not to be tortured, so they just harried him for hours on end, keeping him awake by shouting and shining the light in his face. He fainted several times, and they brought him round again in not too brutal a manner. Night was falling when they took him back to Giskes's lair. He had not talked, but he was at breaking-point and so weak that he flopped about on the back seat of the army car.

He woke up in his cell to find Giskes standing there, in uniform this time. Lauwers had held out against the interrogation by the Gestapo men just because they had interrogated him. He had turned a deaf ear, played the fool with May and his assistants, because they had kept their distance, had deepened the gulf separating captor and prisoner. But Giskes was a very different proposition. Giskes had suggested striking a bargain and Lauwers had discussed the terms. Lauwers had said 'You won't succeed.' He had already given way. It was like pulling at the threads of a knitted garment – pull at one, and all the rest start coming undone.

Lauwers was worn out. He asked for coffee and something to eat. The major gave a short command.

While taking nourishment in this *Abwehr* cell which had become a little haven for him, agent Hubertus Lauwers, code name RLS, realised that he could retreat no farther—a glance at Giskes's stony face was enough – and that he had to accept or refuse the bargain. A sentence often repeated by his instructor at Birmingham suddenly came to mind: 'You can tell them everything – everything, you understand – even your code. But die rather than reveal your security check.' Lauwers knew in himself that the reason why he had not given his code was to see just how long he, the radio operator weak in physique but strong in morale, could hold out. But London couldn't care less whether he revealed his code or not. They had told him so.

'I think,' Giskes said, 'that the time has come for you to make up your mind.'

Lauwers gulped down the last of his black-bread sandwich and nodded agreement.

The cold weather was over. The heavy falls of snow in early March had all disappeared in the past two days. Lauwers had never seen Farenheitsstraat as it was now – clean, hardly damp even, and with heaps of grit and sand stacked every hundred yards or so. The light blue sky was so bright that it hurt his eyes. Lauwers could hardly believe that it was here, in this dirty red building, that he had worked for many weeks, always with his back turned to Teller's frank and open gaze. The house was tall and like any ordinary, middle-class Dutch house, not at all like a hideout.

Lauwers was taken up to the first floor. The room had not changed. The furniture, which had been searched and moved about on the night of the arrest, was all back in place. Yet it did not seem the same room, the one where he had lived through so much excitement and anxiety, so many feverish moments of joy when London replied to his signals. And only two days had passed since his arrest! But now it was full day, spring-like, and the room was no longer an ice-box. The Germans had lit the stove, and the comfortable warmth had driven all mystery from the room.

Lieutenant Heinrichs was seated at Teller's table with some sheets of paper in front of him. He seemed to be absorbed in some calculation. Lauwers saw him underline three figures, copy them on to another sheet, then continue with more groups of three. Every few seconds he referred to a small piece of squared paper on his left. It was the paper with one of the messages that Lauwers had not had time to send.

'He's bluffing,' Lauwers still thought. 'It takes hours to break a code. He'll never do it.'

Only two days ago he had been where the young Nazi was sitting. Previously, whenever he had thought of himself being captured, he had not imagined this heart-rending sacrilege, to see the enemy using his equipment, his paper and pencil, and the table which he had come to look upon as his own. Major Giskes was sitting in the corner, silently playing with the Morse key of Lauwers's transmitter. He must have known that Lauwers was suffering by this silent manner of humiliating him. But the mute torture did not last long, alas.

Heinrichs suddenly looked up from his work and said, 'I've just discovered that the *Prinz Eugen* is at Schiedam.'

'Is that it, Lieutenant Lauwers?' asked Giskes, still playing with the key.

The truth flashed upon Lauwers, and with it came a searing stab of despair. Why had he not realised it sooner? That man Ridderhoff, who Giskes said had been feeding false information to Takonis, had made out the message himself. What an atrocious game! Giskes had not lied to him: for weeks past, he had unknowingly been working for the Germans. His security check apart, he was completely in their power. The bargain that Giskes had proposed did not mean a thing. In all probability he had thought it up in order to break Lauwers's morale, just for that.

'You win,' said Lauwers. Now he could not wait to see Heinrichs work the transmitter, so that the British should learn of his capture. In Lauwers's tired state of mind he imagined that the radio operators in London were waiting only to hear from him. He visualised a dozen signallers, besides a number of women auxiliary telegraphists, all with their headphones on and waiting for *the* message from the continent, the signal from RLS.

But it was not yet time. There were still some minutes to go before his scheduled transmission.

Giskes stopped playing with the Morse key and carried the transmitter over to the table.

'I'm going to show that I trust you,' he said to Lauwers. 'You will work the set yourself. Lieutenant Heinrichs will, of course, keep check on you. I know I'm taking a tremendous risk, but I'd rather do that. Let's say that I've got my own particular reasons for it.'

Giskes's 'particular reasons' had nothing mysterious about about them. Every radio operator had his own style, an individual touch and rhythm on the Morse key. This was called his 'handwriting', and enabled him to be identified at the receiving end. Lauwers had a slow and somewhat stumbling style (he always paused before certain words) which defied imitation. Giskes thought that the British, whom he imagined paid great attention to detail and, especially, had amazing powers of intuition, would soon discover the deception if Heinrichs operated the transmitter instead of Lauwers. The Dutchman realised all this, and it confirmed what he had suspected from the start – that Giskes feared London would break off all contact, whereas if London continued to reply more agents from Britain would fall into the trap he had ready for them. Giskes had not proposed a bargain this time. He had not said to Lauwers, 'I suggest that you work the set yourself.' For the first time, he had given an order to agent RLS. All benevolence had vanished. The military machine in Giskes had taken over from the goodhearted major who so well understood the agonising problems of captured agents. A shiver went through Lauwers. In any case, he would be shot one day soon; so would Takonis. What reason was there for them to be spared? If he refused to work the set, he would only bring the end nearer. Lauwers was not afraid of death, nor hardly afraid of torture. So he could rebel, tell them he would never turn traitor. But there was no sense in that, for by transmitting himself and *omitting his security check* he would automatically warn London.

Lauwers's scheduled time was near. Two of the major's men had plugged in the transmitter and earthed it. Heinrichs began searching for the frequency.

'What is your call sign?' asked Giskes.

'RLS,' said Lauwers. 'I thought you knew it.'

'I believe it's followed by a number?'

'Yes, 1672. Twice.'

Giskes signed to his men, and two of them pushed Lauwers towards the table. He sat down, then asked for a cigarette; Giskes gave him a whole packet. Heinrichs slipped the little Morse key under his hand. Lauwers had the greatest difficulty in concealing his feelings. He was about to contact London, they would know there that he had been captured, they would stop sending agents (or would arrange for other dropping zones), and he would not see any more like Takonis in the corridors, no more Tellers would be hustled into Gestapo cars.

It was not quite 1800 hours when he was handed the headphones. He heard Heinrichs say, 'Get the frequency', and was about to slip on the headphones when he felt Giskes's hand on his right shoulder. He turned and saw a tight-lipped, set smile on the major's face, a calmly cynical face.

'And naturally,' said Giskes, 'you won't forget your security check!'

At that moment, death seemed most desirable to Lauwers. Just before leaving England, he had been given two cyanide pills, two tiny translucent balls, concealed in the false bottom of a box of matches. But, being a religious man and disapproving of suicide, he had thrown the box down a drain the day after he had been dropped into Holland. Now, hearing Giskes's words, he regretted this act. (However, the Germans would have found the box when they searched him.) In contrast to the turmoil within him, everyone standing around seemed quite relaxed. Heinrichs was playing with a nail-file as he leaned over Lauwers's shoulder, and Giskes was humming a little tune. Lauwers sensed that a great weight had been lifted from them.

'I don't know what you mean by security check,' Lauwers said.

'All right, I'll tell you,' Giskes replied amiably. 'You always include a mistake in your message, and always the same kind of mistake, and this proves that your message is genuine. If the mistake is left out, London concludes that you are no longer free. It's simple but effective. Lieutenant Lauwers, you'll never make me believe that you sent messages without including a security check. All your colleagues have one.'

Poor Lauwers. There was now no way out for the frail Dutch agent. He was up against the wall now, and could blame only himself for having got to this stage. From being a secret hero, alone in his glory, he had become a traitor, nothing less, and all in the space of forty-eight hours. He went red with the shame of it, and felt beads of sweat on his forehead. He had only thirty seconds to think of what to do. He could stand up and throw his headphones on the table, declare that they could kill or torture him, but that he was not going through with it. (The Germans were looking at him confidently, like men who had seen other agents, tougher than Lauwers, give in and cooperate.) There was nothing for it – he would try a last trick, a pitiful ruse of an animal at bay, nothing better than a schoolboy's diddle.

'Well, yes,' he said, 'I do make a mistake. Between groups of Morse, I send STIP instead of STOP.'

'Is that all?' exclaimed Giskes. 'Just STIP instead of STOP?' Giskes considered this. It seemed much too simple, and yet in view of the large number of agents sent to the continent and the short time allowed for their training, it was quite conceivable that anything complicated had been avoided. He looked at Lauwers. He did not like him very much, he would rather have dealt with a big brute who could be broken down suddenly, turned in once, who would not have caused him to waste time evaluating the moral aspect of things. Lauwers was probably lying . . . he was certainly lying! Now it was Giskes's turn to be in a dilemma. If he did not accept Lauwers's admission, he could attempt nothing – he was stuck.

'If you're lying, it'll be the worse for you!' he said. 'I've done everything I could to save you.'

'I'm not lying,' Lauwers told him.

He slipped on the headphones and tried to make contact with London. It did not take him very long. With his nose close to the set, he sent off the two fabricated messages that Ridderhoff had given Takonis. Heinrichs had put on headphones too; he was noting each STIP and also checking that Lauwers stuck strictly to the text. He found no discrepancies; Lauwers seemed to be playing the game. His touch on the key was clean and direct, though it betrayed signs of strain now and again; but you could not expect too much from Lauwers that evening.

He could not get over having taken in the major so easily. His real security check was quite different – he had to make an error after every sixteenth letter. This was the first time he had not done so. It was therefore quite simple : at the receiving end, they would realise he was transmitting under enemy control. The thought of it filled him with pride, for singlehanded he had duped the *Abwehr* and Gestapo combined. He would die for it quite soon, of course; as soon as the British realised that his radio post had been 'burned' they would cut the link, and Lauwers would be nothing but a little saboteur, of no use whatever, soon to end up in a ditch at dawn one morning. But Lauwers was full of pride and not at all afraid.

It had taken him less than ten minutes to send the two messages. The Germans had looked on in silence. He felt like a pianist giving a recital to a gathering of music-lovers. Several times he noticed Heinrichs glance at him understandingly (after all, they were both radio operators). As for Giskes, he was probably regretting that he had put the fate of such an important operation (the most important he had ever embarked on) into the nicotine-stained hands – not at all clean in fact – of this young saboteur. But, there, he had had no choice.

Lauwers took off his headphones and turned to Giskes. 'I've finished. They'll send a reply in a few minutes. I take it that this gentleman' (indicating Heinrichs) 'doesn't need me any more?'

As if he were a private who had just performed some heroic

action, Lauwers assumed a slightly insolent manner. They could hardly object to that. And this was something else that Giskes did not like – Lauwers appeared far too pleased with himself. Only fifteen minutes earlier, Lauwers had hardly been able to conceal his nervousness. Now he appeared quite at ease, smoking a cigarette with obvious enjoyment. Even the most unscrupulous traitors did not behave like that. As soon as they had sent their messages, they paced up and down like caged beasts . . . they were afraid of what the future might hold. Why was Lauwers behaving differently?

Heinrichs had taken Lauwers's place in front of the set and was waiting with the headphones on, while Giskes stood behind, easing his legs and making his riding-boots squeak. If Lauwers had lied to him and had used a false security check, the British would send some vague reply and probably ask for the messages to be repeated. That had happened each time they had suspected a *Funkspiel*, a radio set being played back.

Heinrichs gave a start and clapped a hand to his headphones. 'The reply's coming,' he said, and began to jot down groups of letters. It was a very brief signal. He turned to Giskes. 'They say the messages have been received and understood. That's all.'

On 9 March 1942, Thijs Takonis was nothing more than a prisoner, cut off from the world, his friends and his SOE chiefs. He was of no use to anyone, not even to the Germans who had captured him, as he was not a radio operator and so could not be 'turned'. However, Giskes had asked Schreieder to deal cautiously with him, as with Lauwers. It was the big opportunity for the *Kriminalrat* to prove that he preferred to act as an Intelligence officer, in concert with the *Abwehr* major, than as a police officer. To Giskes's great surprise, for he thought Schreieder could never resist the pleasure of bringing a case to a close, the Gestapo chief had taken the risk of sinning by omission and had put the Lauwers and Takonis files away under lock and key. This meant that the RLS case would not be sent to a higher level, and that while the operation continued neither of the two men would be handed over to Rauter for slaughter.

Lauwers and Takonis were being kept in separate cells at Scheveningen prison. Cold air smelling of the sea was wafted in through the narrow fanlight. They had not had a chance to speak to each other since their arrest, but Takonis knew (for Giskes had been quick to tell him) that Lauwers had transmitted under German control after two days of little more than token resistance. Takonis knew that torture had not been necessary, and he was probably thinking that Hubertus was a dirty little traitor and regretting ever having been his friend. Lauwers would have given ten years of his life for Takonis to know the truth – that on 8 March 1942, SOE agent 1672, call signal RLS, had sent two messages under German control but had *omitted his security check*. His instructors at the various training schools had frequently impressed upon him the great importance of security checks. He had been told – and the words still rang in his head – 'The security check is the only means we have of verifying whether you are still free.' So there could be no doubt whatever that London knew he had been captured. And the fact that London had replied with the usual acknowledgement – 'message received and understood' – was undoubtedly to give themselves time to think of the next move. If they had abruptly broken the link they would have been sending Lauwers to face the firing squad straight away. This was what Lauwers would have liked to explain to Takonis.

On the morning of 9 March Lauwers was feeling more confident than ever. He had tricked Giskes quite easily and was no longer impressed by him. When the major entered his cell wearing the same tweed suit as before and looking more relaxed than on the previous morning, Lauwers had no qualms about the day ahead.

An hour later, Giskes and Lauwers left the prison in a grey Mercedes. Lauwers was glad to have only the major as his bodyguard. Despite the handcuffs – which did not trouble him – he felt he was in touch with freedom.

All those who fell into Giskes's snares have said the same thing – he brought you a whiff of a strange friendliness, complied with your wishes and allowed you glimpses of familiar places. He was, moreover, very free with his cigarettes and had a good stock of dirty jokes, for use at the right moment. That was the artistry of the man – he paid heed to the intervals between the acts of a drama of which he was the stage manager. But the heavy price of this familiarity could be read in his birdlike eyes. He had no equal in the manner of stressing an awful threat in a good-natured way.

The Mercedes did not take them to Teller's house (Lauwers never went back there again) but to the *Abwehr* headquarters, the Citadel. Giskes took off the handcuffs at the entrance to the underground passage, then led his prisoner along a corridor for about twenty yards and into a room which seemed at first glance to be a school laboratory filled with busy students. Then Lauwers recognised Heinrichs, bent over his coding. A dozen soldiers were sitting in front of big radio sets, much better ones than the poor instrument on which Lauwers had sent his messages. A year's training and all manner of sufferings had brought him to this, thirty feet underground and among field-green uniforms, in the keeping of a devilish major. . . . He gave a shudder, all the same. He was surprised to find that not a single one of these Germans treated him with the scorn usually reserved for an enemy turned traitor. Heinrichs and the youthful signallers spoke to him as if he were one of them. He was no one's prisoner . . . unless he was only Giskes's.

As on the previous day, but at a different table, he was given a chair. Heinrichs had already coded the messages to be sent, and had inscribed them on a large sheet of squared paper with the heading of Army Headquarters; he now placed this beside the transmitter. Giskes put a full packet of Turkish cigarettes on the table, before Lauwers had even asked for a smoke.

In less than an hour's time, Giskes and the others would know where they stood. Lauwers was thinking that there were two ways in which the British might react. They could refuse to accept his signals, leaving him to his fate. He knew this was part of the risks of secret warfare. Another sentence repeated a hundred times by his instructors came to mind: 'From the moment you're captured, you cease to exist for us. You're as good as dead.' It was more than likely that London would break all contact with him. He was prepared for that, and bore no one ill-will.

The other eventuality was that London would reply as though nothing untoward had occurred. They would play a double game, letting Giskes believe that they had been duped. Lauwers had heard this often happened, but there was nothing to prove it was not just a story. He found it difficult to believe that they had the time and the means to maintain contact with a radio post that was 'burnt', as they called it, just to save the life of some unfortunate agent (while in England, Lauwers had had an inkling of the cynicism prevailing in the secret services). At most, if they saw some strategical reason. . . . But what was Holland, more precisely Lauwers's small area, the rudimentary Van den Berg network, in the overall strategy of the world war? For the third time since his arrest, Hubertus Lauwers saw himself put against a wall, to-morrow perhaps. He felt a new fear coming over him, very different from his fear when making a parachute jump – an icy tingle was creeping up his spine.

When the time came for Lauwers to make contact with London, the officers and men gathered round his table. Heinrichs had put headphones on and was listening in with Lauwers. They could hear scraps of Morse, bits of messages cutting across one another, probably coming from all over Europe. Lauwers was slowly turning the knob, trying to tune in, a little to the left, then a little to the right. He thought for a moment that he had it, then tried a little to the left again. He saw Giskes glance at his watch. London ought to have come through some minutes ago. . . . This was the end. Lauwers was convinced of it now—the British wanted nothing more to do with his radio post. He was 'dead'. He turned the knob a little to the left again, telling himself this was the last time before taking off his headphones and saying to the major that he couldn't understand what was the matter but it was impossible to get them this evening. And he would try to explain, hoping to survive a little longer, that it often happened because there were so many clandestine transmitters and they used frequencies which were very close together, so there was absolutely no need to worry. But then, suddenly, a long low whistling filled the headphones.

'You've got them,' said Heinrichs. 'Now begin . . .'

Lauwers tapped out his call sign three times, and at once received the signal to start sending. The message at his side was much longer than the previous ones. It contained fabricated information of a most precise nature – troop movements in northern Brabant, the strength of the Luftwaffe squadrons stationed at Eindhoven, the construction of a U-boat base south of Rotterdam, and more besides. Giskes was smiling down at Lauwers, probably imagining British Intelligence officers moving little flags around on a huge map.

Giskes was not entirely free of anxiety, however. He realised that the British decoders had not yet had time to check thoroughly the messages sent by Lauwers the previous day, and he would have to wait another day or two before feeling certain that Lauwers had revealed his true security check.

Lauwers finished transmitting, took off his headphones and left Heinrichs to wait for the reply from London. The Dutchman was red in the face and perspiring freely. He suddenly felt giddy from so much conflicting emotion, and asked the major if he could walk about the room.

'Please do,' said Giskes.

Lauwers strode up and down, one hand behind his back and the other clutching a cigarette. He did not know what to think now, he dare not imagine. It was quite possible that London would not reply at all, for he had again omitted his real security check.

But Heinrichs suddenly signed to Giskes, then seized a pencil and began taking down the signal. Heinrichs wrote each letter on a large sheet of squared paper. Giskes, looking over his shoulder, chafed at being unable to understand the coded message as it came through. There was no longer any reason for him to hide his anxiety. Lauwers had done what was required, and knew that on his 'loyalty' depended the success of an operation unique in the history of counter-espionage.

Heinrichs at last took off his headphones. 'I think,' he said (and only in quite exceptional circumstances did Heinrichs take the liberty of expressing an opinion), 'I think this message is very important.'

'You can write it out later,' Giskes said in a voice like a whiplash. 'Tell me the gist of it at once.'

Heinrichs stood to attention and read the message in a loud voice, as though making a speech.

'Message received and understood. . . . Try making it shorter. . . . Regarding dropping zone chosen by Thijs OK. . . . Abor will be dispatched with arms containers 25 March. . . . Prepare reception committee. . . . Further instructions follow later. . . . Message ends.'

Lauwers thought he was going out of his mind. *The British were sending messages!* By agreeing to Giskes's bargain he had been caught in the mesh. By transmitting under German control he had become, despite all his efforts, an agent for the enemy.

4

Hope Revived

They had fastened Takonis's hands behind his back with a pair of large, old-fashioned handcuffs which were locked with a kind of door-key. When he sat down he got stabbing pains in the small of his back after about fifteen minutes. The pains were just as bad if he curled up on the bench, but he got them between his ribs and at his elbows. It was tolerable only when he stood up, but eventually he needed to sleep, and then he had to sit or lie down.

Takonis had not talked, not even told his name, to the brutish May, nor to Inspector Bayer, who was perhaps more humane. The Germans knew, thanks to Ridderhoff, that his name was Takonis. But that was all they had been able to find out about the 'tall half-caste'. The day after his arrest (at Arnhem; German and Dutch police had surrounded the house where he was staying for the night) he had attacked the Dutch jailer who brought his food and tried to strangle him. This was the reason for Takonis being hand-cuffed.

On 10 March Major Giskes went for the third time to visit Lauwers in his cell. He was on the first floor, where the 'political' prisoners were kept. Behind each cell door were one or more men who had been arrested as hostages or members of the Re-sistance and who expected to die before very long – Rauter's 'justice' knew neither mercy nor pardon. Lauwers's cell was right at the end of the long corridor. Giskes was followed all the way by a clamour from the condemned prisoners, by kicks and bangs on the doors, shouts and insults and defiant, patriotic songs. The *Abwehr* major was not exactly annoyed or disgusted, but glad that he had nothing to do with the repressive measures carried out by his black-clad colleagues, measures which were approved by practically the whole of the German Army.

The tumult was greater than ever that morning. Ten leading citizens of Amsterdam had been shot at dawn, because on the previous day a German soldier had been attacked and killed in the street by a young Dutchman (who got away). The remaining prisoners were yelling their hatred, beating it out on the pipes, with a mad abandon that came from knowing that their death was near. The jailer accompanying Giskes banged on the cell doors as they passed, shouting back automatically, 'Pipe down! Keep quiet in there!' The major wished they could all be freed (or strangled) there and then, the whole lot of them. Anything to shut them up! He had almost reached the end of the corridor when he came to a cell whose door had been replaced by iron bars – a cage holding a wild animal.

'Who is this man?' said Giskes, stopping.

'His name's Takonis,' replied the jailer.

This was the first time that Giskes had seen him. He was just as he had been described to him – tall, swarthy, with long straight hair.

'I will not have a man held by my orders tied up like an animal. Unfasten him!'

Giskes said later that when the handcuffs were taken off, Takonis thanked him with a bow in the Oriental manner. The major omitted to add that Takonis also spat in his face. He did not dwell on it, knowing that blackguards and honest men, heroes and cowards are easily tied up, but never madmen or saints. And there could be no doubt in this case. Takonis's appearance fitted the man; he looked like a bronzed figure of Christ on the cross, with a face deeply marked by anger and weariness – one of the just. Giskes, disregarding what the Dutch jailer might think, said that Takonis was not to be punished for his insolence.

'Your attitude is stupid, and it won't do you any good,' Giskes contented himself with saying to the prisoner. 'We know all about you, and what your mission was here.' Then he added a little spitefully: 'The agent Abor will be dropped at Zoutkampt on the twenty-fifth, at the place you chose yourself. We shall capture him when he lands. Goodbye, Mr Takonis.'

Giskes went into Lauwers's cell. The Dutchman had spent a restless night; although he had eaten little, he had smoked a lot. And he was calmer in his mind. He had no doubt now that his two messages had been understood, and wondered whether he had included his real security check after all, instinctively. But then he remembered—he had deliberately refrained from counting the letters. He was quite sure he had not counted every sixteenth letter, he would have sworn it on the Bible. Why, then, had they replied as though nothing was wrong? Why had they given Giskes, in a single message, more information than he could have dragged out of the worst of traitors? Then Lauwers remembered that messages from the continent were not received in London by radio. The radio station was somewhere in the western counties, and every evening a despatch rider took the day's messages to London, where, it was said, they were decoded the following morning by some people at the War Office. Practically no decision about them was taken for three days. Lauwers recalled all he had heard about the infallibility of Intelligence, that national sport of the English, and began to take hope.

However, Giskes was looking more satisfied than Lauwers had ever seen him.

'Lieutenant Lauwers,' he said, 'I've given much thought to the matter of conscience that working for the German Army must be causing you. And I've decided to do all in my power to ensure that neither you nor any of your comrades are brought before a military court. I'm sure you know what that implies.'

'I do,' said Lauwers.

There was no connection between his 'matter of conscience' and having his life spared. Lauwers thought the major's remarks were inappropriate, but made no comment.

For the third time, Giskes was fetching him from prison to go and 'work'. But this time Giskes took him to a villa that the *Abwehr* had requisitioned in Park Street, Scheveningen, close to the sea front. The car was the same as before, with the same driver. Lauwers breathed deeply as they drove along by the sea. This change of air, so soon after leaving his prison cell, was like having an oxygen mask clamped over his face, and it made him feel uneasy. Giskes had not handcuffed him, counting on his own great strength and the small Walther pistol in the pocket of his jacket to cope with any eventuality.

Heinrichs was waiting for them, as usual now, with two army coding clerks. The house belonged to a wireless enthusiast, but the man was either dead or a refugee. There were no signs of recent habitation in the brown-walled dining-room. Lauwers worked the transmitter as on the two previous occasions, but then asked if he could listen with Lieutenant Heinrichs for London to reply.

The message concerned the despatch of the agent 'Abor'. Because of the moon, he would not be dropped until the 27th. The evenly-spaced groups of Morse which would have filled Lauwers with great hopes if he had been free, now only brought him deep anxiety. He watched Heinrichs decoding the whole message. They again told RLS to keep his messages short, but they were in general most satisfied, congratulated him and asked him to convey the staff's thanks to 'long Thijs' for his activities.

Lauwers read and re-read the text, but could find no hint of any connivance, no indication that they were aware of the grim and awful truth. Admittedly, they had put back the date by two days, but that meant nothing. Lauwers knew that the British frequently put back operations, for reasons best known to themselves. However, if the tales he had heard at the training schools were true, it was not unusual for them to have shown no reaction as yet. Lauwers did not know what to think.

The following day it was not Giskes but one of his officers, a Lieutenant Huntemann, who fetched Lauwers from his cell. This meant that Lauwers's treachery had become an accomplished fact, Giskes now had better things to do than supervise the small-time agent whom he had turned. Huntemann was a big, fair-haired, rough-hewn countryman who never deviated an inch from his line of duty – and so put the handcuffs on Lauwers. Hubertus was feeling lost, being cut off from London – where they had still not grasped the facts – and also from Giskes, with whom he had made a bargain. Despite having four Germans round him, Lauwers felt more alone than he had ever been.

Heinrichs had ready a message dictated by Giskes which referred to the reception of the agent 'Abor'. The *Abwehr* major had decided to push his luck and make sure that the link with London was firmly secured by questioning the decision to drop the agent at Zoutkampt. It was too near a large town, and he suggested another spot in the rough country north of Steenwijk. Lauwers was about to tap out this message when he mustered all his courage, and said :

'I'm not going to send this, I'll never send anything again.'

Neither Heinrichs nor Huntemann, let alone Wuhr or his pal

Kupp, took it upon himself to persuade Lauwers. They might have tried with another man, and would certainly have beaten him up. But Lauwers was Giskes's personal prey, the shock-weapon of his own little war. No one wanted to risk upsetting the major's plans. They merely put away the transmitter and had Lauwers taken back to prison.

An hour later, Giskes entered his cell, wearing uniform, and made a little speech.

'Now understand this – with or without your help, we shall get our hands on the man we've been told is to be dropped. You know that, don't you? You know the means we have? Well then, think over your decision. I've already told you that I'm here in Holland to prevent civil war breaking out. I can do that only by seizing the men and weapons which your chiefs in London drop into Holland. That's how it is. That's war, and I'm at war, Lieutenant Lauwers. Now listen to this. I've nearly got the OKW, the German High Command, to agree that all the agents captured during my operation shall have their lives spared, beginning with you and your friend Takonis.' (Lauwers had still not admitted that he knew Takonis.) 'But on one condition. And you know what it is.'

Lauwers had not moved or spoken. He was listening. For the first time, he had refused to take a cigarette from Major Giskes.

'You know what I mean,' the latter repeated in a louder voice. 'You must continue to transmit under our control, that's all. Otherwise, if you're of no use to us, I can't save your life, or anyone else's. It's quite simple. An intelligent man like you ought to understand.'

It was indeed simple, like all effective blackmail. Lauwers had no need to hear the terms, he had known them from the start. He had rebelled only to prove to himself that he still could; and because he had wondered how the Germans would take it. Now he knew. Giskes had given another turn to the vice and had made the situation clear. If Lauwers stopped transmitting for the *Abwehr*, all his comrades would die. And so would he.

Just before five in the afternoon, Lauwers was again placed in front of his transmitter, faced with his responsibilities. Since his capture, his relations with London had imperceptibly become a dialogue. He sent a message, London replied to it, he sent another message. He and London had begun a discussion, and this was exactly what Giskes had wanted. And London, as on the previous day and the one before that, did not understand. Yet Lauwers had *never once* included his proper security check!

At six in the evening of 25 March 1942, Lauwers was about to transmit under German control for the tenth time. The agent 'Abor' and several containers were to be parachuted two nights later. As Lauwers sat down in front of his set, a Dutchman at a camp somewhere in England was packing up his 'personal effects' before handing them to his instructor. He would have been told to write on a piece of cardboard, to be attached to the handle of his suitcase, 'the name of the person to be informed in the event of disappearance'. In an hour's time he would say goodbye to his comrades, and then he would be driven to the small airfield in south-east England which was used by the special services. There he would spend two days on a 'finishing course', learning his codes and security check by heart, and the names and addresses of safe friends in Holland to be contacted if he found no 'reception committee' on the dropping-ground. One of those friends would certainly be 'long Thijs'. Just before getting into the plane, the agent would be given his false identity papers and a box of matches or a cork containing the poison pills, which were made to taste of violets (was death any the sweeter?).

Lauwers could think only of this poor fellow, whom he might even know. For a moment he felt like picking up the transmitter and smashing it on the floor. But what good would that do? There was no loophole in Giskes's odious argument. In any case, they were going to capture the agent.

It seemed to Lauwers that London was waiting impatiently for his message that evening, so easily did he make contact. Giskes had given him a very short message to send, merely confirming that all was ready for the parachute drop on 27 March.

The British took less than a minute to send a reply. The two lines of text were clear and curt, devoid of any feeling:

'Agent Abor ill stop parachute drop 27 March postponed *sine die* stop message ends.'

Lauwers took a deep breath. The great searing weight was lifted from him. London had understood.

5

Collapse

Everyone in the prison, petty thieves and hostages, brothel-keepers and spies, Resistance members, swindlers, and 'those who were in for nothing at all', all knew that Lauwers was a traitor, and Lauwers knew what they – many of whom, if threatened, would have betrayed their parents, friends and mistresses – were saying about him.

Lauwers was having a foretaste of hell. What could he say in reply? He could have explained it to them, for, as in prisons everywhere, the pipes along the floors were the prisoners' telephone system. They tapped out their hatred, their scorn and their insults in Morse, slowly and carefully, separating the groups so that the message could be clearly understood. 'Lauwers is a traitor.... He has given everyone away.... Pass it along.... Lauwers is a shit.... I repeat, Lauwers is a shit.... He is working for the Gestapo.... Pass it along.'

What could he say in reply? He could explain steadily: 'I have not given my real security check.... Pass it along.... I have taken the Germans in.... London has understood.... The agent Abor will not be dropped, thanks to me.... Pass it along.' But what would be the use? It was too long, too awkward. And how many of them, apart from Takonis, knew what a security check was? The common criminals on the floor below were the most virulent. Brothel-keepers were accusing Saint Lauwers of a crime he had not committed, burglars were banging out their contempt of him on the water pipes. But what did it matter to him? Despite the bangings, Lauwers had a good night's sleep. 'Abor' would never be dropped, he kept telling himself. The British would send a plane to drop two or three containers, they would keep up the pretence for a few days, and then it would all be over – the end of the game, the end of Lauwers and of Takonis. That he should be taken for a swine by a handful of idiots, cowards and criminals, with a few brave fellows among them, certainly grieved him, but it did not affect his pride in having warned London.

When he woke in the morning he began to think that appearances would be against him. No one would clear his name. Still, he had no wife or child. The bourgeois Lauwers dynasty would end with him, and nobody would have the shame of bearing his name. All the same, it was hard. Nobody would ever know the truth. . . .

There was complete silence around him: the pipes were no longer vibrating. For a moment, he had the feeling of being the only prisoner in the building. But, of course, it was still very early and the others were all asleep. Later, after the coffee had been brought round, a jailer would take him out for exercise, by himself (he had to be kept away from the other prisoners), like an important captive. And all along the corridor the prisoners would insult him, shouting this time, for they knew whose were the short unsteady steps along the steel floor at eight o'clock or soon after.

Lauwers wanted Takonis to know the truth at all costs. The others did not matter, but Takonis, one of the just, must not die believing that Lauwers was a traitor. He crouched down below the wash basin and started tapping on the widest part of the outflow pipe with his long fingernails.

'Lauwers calling Takonis. . . . Pass it along. . . .'

A flow of insults reached him almost at once. The traitor Lauwers was told not to disturb the sleep of people who had given no one away, who did not work for the Gestapo. But Lauwers repeated his message, tapping as carefully as if working his transmitter.

'Lauwers calling Takonis. . . . Pass it along.' And he continued, 'I have not betrayed anyone. . . . Takonis. . . .' Other prisoners replied with a clamour on the pipes. But Lauwers kept tapping away. 'Takonis. . . . I have not betrayed anyone. . . . I did not give my security check. . . . Takonis . . . I am not a traitor. . . .'

The others gradually ceased, tired out by their own hatred or because they vaguely realised that the matter was beyond them. Lauwers repeated that he was no traitor four or five times, then the silence grew. He sat down, feeling hopeless, while the early daylight filtered into the cell.

Then suddenly, and not to his surprise, the pipe along the floor began to vibrate evenly with Morse. 'I knew it,' Takonis was replying.

It must have been about one o'clock in the morning, on 28 March 1942. Giskes, Wuhr, Huntemann, Kupp, and two soldiers with submachine guns dangling against their stomachs, were waiting among some stunted willows on the edge of a triangular field. Schreieder was there too. The Gestapo had come in strength, as usual, and there were at least fifteen SS stamping their feet and muffled up to the eyebrows. Across the fields could be seen a few lights flickering in the blackout at Steenwijk.

For the second time, *Kriminalrat* Schreieder was risking his career by collaborating with Major Giskes. If something went wrong, if the expected RAF aircraft dropped bombs instead of the containers as promised, and SS men were killed, then Schreieder would have much explaining to do. He could expect awful sanctions to be taken against him. He would be lucky to get away with a posting to the Russian front. In short, Schreieder was in a very bad humour. He stepped across to the *Abwehr* major.

'You're quite certain about this business, aren't you? If anything goes wrong, remember I've warned you – I shall deny having anything to do with you. You realise I'm taking a terrible risk in helping you.'

Giskes felt just as anxious. He saw himself being denounced to Rauter and having to appeal to Canaris for help – and all because a little black-uniformed policeman was suddenly scared of going through with it. Giskes fumed inwardly, but merely said with a shrug of the shoulders: 'I've already told you—nothing will go wrong.'

The SS and the *Abwehr* men scattered across the field; they were all carrying torches, and some had instinctively drawn their revolvers, clutching them in the left hand. The plane was soon heard approaching from the north-west; Giskes could tell it was British from the sound of its engines. Wuhr flashed his torch, and two SS did the same. Suddenly the aircraft was right over them, zooming across the field at tree-top height. Several men dropped to the ground, then picked themselves up, plastered with mud. The plane circled the field, flying a little higher. The pilot must have seen the flashing torches, for he reduced speed to the lowest limit, it seemed, and three objects darker than the night came hurtling down.

They were not bombs. The waiting Germans saw three parachutes open, steadying the containers before they hit the ground with dull thuds. The men all ran towards them; they were huge, and one was standing upright with its nose buried in the sticky earth. 'Halt!' cried an SS *Scharführer*, a daring youngster who seemed most knowledgeable, some specialist perhaps. 'Keep away!' he shouted, peremptorily waving back the officers and men. He walked slowly towards the huge object stuck in the ground. The others let him get on with it; he felt round the object like a blind man fingering a work of art, then put his ear to various places. No one made a sound. Despite his junior rank, the young SS had given orders which brooked no argument, the lives of all depended on him. The men in black and in field-green waited in an ever-widening circle; the *Scharführer* soon found himself alone in the field, listening intently to one container after another, while Giskes shone a torch on him from a distance. The minutes dragged by, heavy with thoughts of these three dark objects which might be delayed-action bombs. After a time – no one could have said how long – the *Scharführer* waved his gloved hands in an expansive negative sign to the others. They drew near, while he stepped back into the ranks, as it were, his authority at an end. He had risked his life for fifteen minutes of absolute power.

Nothing had gone wrong. Schreieder was rubbing his hands – not so much because of the cold as because he was again co-partner in the operation. And he began calling Major Giskes his *Lieber Kamerad* once more.

Soon after daybreak, Lauwers was brought from his cell and taken to the Binnenhoff. He had asked if he could see the night's haul, for he wanted to be quite sure. . . .

Schreieder, Giskes and a few others were in a large shed which had been specially erected in the courtyard. They were standing there in silence. They had been up all night, they had been frightened. Altogether, fifty men and a lorry had been ordered out, and the anti-aircraft battery at Steenwijk had been told not to fire at any enemy plane. And all for this.

Lauwers looked at what was displayed on the ground, at what had been found in the SOE's huge metal surprise packets. There were three dozen Stens (but no magazines for them), which had been placed side by side, thereby making the night's harvest look even more meagre, and 1,000 leaflets with a tricolour line across them, intended for the Resistance in the Drôme *département* of France. Lauwers picked one up and pretended to read it. Probably a rousing call to arms, he thought, judging by the number of exclamation marks.

Lauwers was anxiously wondering what would happen to him and Takonis. Giskes had promised that while they continued to be useful to him, they would not be put on trial, or sent to Germany. But now London had just broken off all contact – and how! Like giving the major a slap in the face.

Giskes gave a little kick at the pile of leaflets and looked at Lauwers with hard, metallic eyes.

'This can only be due to an error in despatch, wouldn't you say, Lieutenant Lauwers?'

'Yes, indeed. An error in despatch.'

That same morning, somewhere in the foothills of the French Alps, between Valence and Gap, a group of young men in lumber-jackets and with guns slung from their shoulders were gloomily trying to make sense of leaflets in Dutch, some message or other from Gerbrandy, the head of the Dutch Government in London. The young men in lumber-jackets, too, must have said 'There's been an error in despatch.' But through clenched teeth.

Schreieder was becoming impatient, hopping from one foot to the other. He was no longer taking part, indeed not! This was the last time he would get mixed up in the *Abwehr's* mad schemes. He had been made to look ridiculous – quite ridiculous! – in front of his men, now standing rigidly in an attitude of respect which they no longer felt.

'Obviously,' he sneered, 'Mr Lauwers sent the messages correctly, *Hein*?'

'Yes, I sent them correctly,' said Lauwers. 'Lieutenant Heinrichs will confirm that.'

Heinrichs was a SS officer. If a mistake had been made, the responsibility fell upon Schreieder's shoulders. In replying as he did, Lauwers had all unknowingly renewed his lease of life. Major Giskes took it as a mark of sympathy (was he so far wrong?). He wanted to know exactly what had happened, and so he had to pretend not to suspect Lauwers. If the Dutchman had double-crossed him, he would do it again: but one day or another he would slip up – and then woe betide him.

'Lieutenant Lauwers,' said the major quietly, 'tell your English friends, if you see them again one day. that there's one principle in secret warfare which must always be observed—order.'

The sheets of paper on the ground were shining like silver where the light fell on them, and the red and blue of the diagonal lines looked like deep violet. The faces of Giskes, Schreieder and the others were pallid and ghostlike, as in a dream. Perhaps Lauwers really was in a dream; but at least it was not a nightmare, for he was sure of one thing – the agent 'Abor' would never be dropped now.

It was seven in the evening, and no one had come to fetch Lauwers from his cell: he would not be going to 'work' that day. He did not go to work the following day either. And when he was brought from his cell on 30 March he was not taken to *Abwehr* headquarters, nor to the house by the sea.

The car was heading south-east from The Hague.

'Where are we going?' Lauwers asked.

'You're being transferred,' was all that the driver replied.

The theological college at Haaren, North Brabant, had been turned into a prison. This had happened quite recently, and the saintly smells of incense and tallow which had been impregnating the walls for the past three hundred years still persisted slightly under the sharp odours of disinfectant and detergents. The parlour was still a parlour, and the monks' cells were still used as cells. A few iron bars had been added, heavier locks put on doors made stronger. But the same peepholes were in use, the same pallets and rough blankets, and the dress of the inmates was much the same.

Most of the prisoners at Haaren had been summarily tried and sentenced. Executions took place at dawn on Fridays, sometimes on Mondays as well. The victims – men sentenced to death or taken as hostages – were led out to the monastery garden, now a prison courtyard, and lined up along a deep ditch. As they were shot, their bodies fell back into the black- gaping earth. When the firing was over, the singing of crazed men, of condemned men gone crazy, took the place of Matins. The older ones nobly sang the *Wilhelmus Lied,* others preferred the *Internationale,* but most of them just bawled out their hate until their voices gave out and ended in sobs and cries.

To make Lauwers think things over, Giskes had placed him on the edge of the deep ditch. The major had only to give an order, and at dawn one Friday or one Monday.... Takonis too had been transferred to Haaren. Lauwers was aware of this, although he had not seen him.

The prisoners communicated over the water pipes, as at Scheveningen. On the very first night Lauwers discovered that his reputation had accompanied him from Scheveningen, if not preceded him. Giskes certainly did things properly! He was woken before dawn by words of hatred being madly tapped out on the lead pipes, and the tone had hardened. 'You've got it coming to you, Lauwers.... Like all traitors.' But they soon got tired of it, each prisoner thinking more of his own imminent death and listening to the sounds in the corridor, looking for signs of some miracle.

They left Lauwers alone the following day. Something very odd was happening. A man's voice penetrated every cell, drowning all other voices, all footsteps and metallic sounds. Another crazed prisoner – yet how talented! – was singing an excerpt from *Lucia di Lammermoor*, the most difficult passage of all. Someone in despair was bringing more tears, though not tears of despair, to the eyes of his fellow-prisoners. He followed with an air from *Figaro*, usually a woman's part. It was so lovely to hear, yet so out of place, almost indecent, there on the threshold of death.

Lauwers knew very little about opera, but he had heard these same airs being sung and hummed not so very long ago. And that voice, so clear and loud but not very manly – he seemed to have heard it before. But when, where? Before the war, or in England? So much had happened in a short space of time. The new arrival next sang an excerpt from *Iphigénie en Tauride*, Act Two – an opera not often heard, rather boring, and technically very difficult. Lauwers thought this stranger than ever, for he had heard the excerpt sung before, though he could not remember when. In his present state of mind, events in the past were all confused. Was it at the Concertgebouw in 1933 or 1934? No, it couldn't have been – he remembered that had been a performance of *Tristan and Isolde*.

The singing stopped. Probably the man was tired – he had been singing for over two hours, almost continuously. The jailers, who were all Dutch, had made no attempt to stop the recital, for while it lasted, the prisoners had at least stopped shouting and yelling. In the silence that followed, the water pipes began to vibrate again. It was not to insult Lauwers this time. The new arrival, according to the traditions of the prison, was explaining how he came to be there, and all in very good Morse.

He had dropped from the skies on the night of 29 March. Before he had time even to struggle out of his parachute-harness, a couple of burly Germans in civilian clothes had seized him and got the handcuffs on him. He had fought wildly, lashing out with his feet, and one of the policemen had collapsed with a yell, holding his crutch. But others had run up and overwhelmed him. They had hit him, hard and precisely, and one of his ribs was probably broken. Later, at the Gestapo offices, they had had a good laugh at his expense, as his raincoat still had the 'Burton' label in it, the Dutch money found in the lining of his jacket had been withdrawn from circulation a year ago, and his identity card was obviously forged by an apprentice. There was nothing more humiliating than hearing their 'Aie! Amateurish! English very negligent!'

Lauwers was lying at full length on the cold floor so as to put his ear close to the pipe. Finally, after sending a few more details, the man gave his name – Baatsen.

Baatsen!

Lauwers saw him as he had known him at Ringway, a tall, lively young man who was made fun of because he was thought to dye his hair. He used to jump and tremble all over if a Sten was fired anywhere near him. He had been nicknamed 'Blond Rita'.

They had often had a chuckle over Baatsen, especially when he was seen crying with fear at the top of the jumping-tower. Everyone had wondered – even Lauwers, who was no athlete – why a man like Baatsen had been accepted for 'special work'. Yet it was the same man who had drawn his revolver when the Germans rushed at him and would have shot Wuhr, if Wuhr had not been the quicker and gripped his wrist hard enough to break it. Yes, Wuhr – for Baatsen had fallen into the hands of Giskes and Schreieder. For, on the evening of 28 March, London had given warning of his arrival. For Baatsen (and a chill ran down Lauwers's spine) *was the agent 'Abor'.*

Giskes had won. London had not understood, and the radio game, the *England Spiel*, was beginning. Operation North Pole, a masterpiece of counter-intelligence work, had got under way.

PART TWO *The Anvil*

6

The Great Round-Up

At first sight, there was nothing to distinguish Antonius Van der Waals from the other blackguards, sometimes well-informed but more often inventors of tales, always despicable and generally avaricious, whom the police everywhere and in all ages have never been able to do without. He was just one informer among many, another V-man (*Vertrauensmann*), as the Germans called them.

Joseph Schreieder spent an hour every morning hearing reports from such men, sorting out and picking from the job-lots of gossip and information that they brought him for a small weekly payment. Schreieder thought that these men must have an urge, a real vocation, to be traitors; for there were other occupations, less dangerous and better paid, cleaner and requiring no special skills, still available to them even at The Hague and in 1942.

At least, Schreieder was not mistaken in the case of Van der Waals. Like Ridderhoff, he too had a face that went with the job —a smooth face with a thick lower lip than hung loosely, downcast eyes with dark rings round them, a broad shiny forehead and protruding ears. He was of medium build, slovenly dressed and dirty. He whispered rather than spoke, and emphasised his words by giving a listless poke upwards with his finger, always the first finger. He undoubtedly had a vocation. It was obvious that Van der Waals had created his part of a traitor as carefully as an actor, and when he had first appeared at the Gestapo office, on 27 April 1941, the *Kriminalrat* almost had him thrown out.

However, Antonius was more than just a layabout – much more, and worse. On 27 April 1941, a German soldier had been shot in a Haarlem street. Rauter had cast the usual bloody shadow of reprisals over the large towns. Many hostages were shot, but the guilty man had not been found. And Van der Waals had gone to tell Schreieder that he could lead him to the terrorist. When

Schreieder asked him what were his reasons, he had coolly replied in his soft voice that he needed the money, that Holland was German by its very nature and therefore people who attacked German soldiers were traitors.

Informers do not usually explain their motives so fully, and Schreieder was intrigued, a little embarrassed too. He was not used to hearing ideological statements from his V-men. He repeated his question. Van der Waals (aged thirty at most) again answered that he needed money and that he was a Germanophile. He added that his real occupation was inventor – he had just perfected a rotor engine – and pianist. He needed money badly in order to equip his own laboratory and to buy a concert piano. Schreieder's first thought was that the man was crazy – 'probably not dangerous, but crazy all the same'.

'I don't like your kind,' Schreieder said.

'I never asked you to like me, Herr Kommissar. I came to do a deal with you, that's all.'

'All right. What's the assassin's name?'

The name was Bierhuys, and, led by Van der Waals, Schreieder had arrested him the following day. For good measure, Van der Waals betrayed the man who had hidden Bierhuys's gun – a priest, Father Joseph Klinger. The two were executed, and Van der Waals was taken on at a monthly salary by the Gestapo. Schreieder became convinced that he was crazy, but he was also the best man that he had ever found for his dirty work.

When Operation North Pole began, Schreieder had a very valuable V-man in Van der Walls. During the intervening months, Antonius had considerably widened his range of contacts (and also improved his technique), and Schreieder had discovered that his private list of informers was better than the Gestapo's. Schreieder did not take offence at this, but waited for a chance to use Van der Waals to good effect – the Gestapo's relations with the *Abwehr* were finely balanced.

Meanwhile, Lauwers had begun transmitting again. Three times a week he was brought from his cell, just before four in the afternoon, and taken to Scheveningen. Giskes, Heinrichs, Wuhr and the others were there to watch him send the messages. Yet 'Abor' had been dropped, and the following night almost a ton of weapons and ammunition had fallen at the Germans' feet. So it could be said that he was a traitor. But he had not once included his real security check. Yet who knew that? More particularly, had anyone noticed it? This thought went round and round in his head. His instructors' words kept coming back to him: 'Die rather than disclose your security check.' They had drummed it into him: 'If you have to, reveal everything, your code and the rest, but never your security check.' He had not imagined it.

He could not sleep at night, and only dropped off in the morning just as the jailer came to take him out for exercise. He was still kept isolated, but neither the Dutch jailers nor the Germans – except Giskes – now treated him with the distant respect given to important prisoners. Besides, he was no longer indispensable; Heinrichs could now imitate his 'handwriting' perfectly. The German had sent a test message, and the British had not noticed anything amiss.

But then, the British noticed so very little. Lauwers racked his brain to find an explanation. Were his messages decoded by someone incompetent? – impossible; the clerks worked as a team and in shifts. Had the system of security checks been replaced by another? – highly unlikely. Was there a traitor at the London end? – if so, who? Lauwers was not very imaginative, and these two or three possibilities went round and round in his head, excluding any others. Besides, his moral standards and unquestioning respect for everything British precluded any idea that it could all be a horrible, bloody masquerade, and that he, Takonis and 'Blond Rita' were being sacrificed to some high-level plan. That was the stuff of novels, and it never occurred to Lauwers. So the question remained. And daily at exercise time a great gulf, a black emptiness, suddenly stretched before him – what use was he?

The other prisoners had stopped threatening him. He had learned over the 'telephone' that Baatsen could make no sense of it either, and bore him no grudge. It was felt on the second floor of Haaren prison that Lauwers's case was far from straightforward. So he was left in peace.

On 27 April 1942, Heinrichs was decoding a message intended for Takonis which had just been received. Lauwers was there in the big room at *Abwehr* headquarters. It was seven in the evening, and he had been brought from Haaren because, as Giskes told him, a very important message might be received from London, 'and in such an event, Lieutenant Lauwers, I prefer to have you

with me'. The major was in one of his high good humours, over-
flowing with cordiality – an expansive mood that Lauwers had
come to dread. He sometimes felt he would sooner have been
handed over to a torturer. Giskes cracked jokes, sent for coffee
and handed round cigarettes. He reminded Lauwers of an enthusiastic scoutmaster leading a sad, bedraggled troop on a country walk.

Heinrichs finished his task and passed the paper to Giskes, who
read the latest instructions from London:

'Go to the tobacconist at The Hague stop ask for Pijl stop message ends.'

This was what the major had been hoping for – the British
were making RLS a focus for other agents! And the British had
just told Giskes what he had been both hoping and fearing since
the first day of the *Funkspiel* – that there were other espionage
and sabotage groups active in Holland. Lauwers, Teller and
Takonis were not the only agents roaming about the Low Countries in search of information. There were other radio operators
sending messages to London.

If Giskes, aided by Schreieder, did not capture these agents,
turn them and play back their sets within a very short time, they
might at any moment warn London of the deception in progress.
And that would be the end of Operation North Pole! That would
mean the collapse of the *England Spiel*, of the radio game! A
great round-up had to be carried out if the *England Spiel* was to
continue. And luck was with Giskes. But he suddenly wondered
whether it was really a stroke of luck that the British should be
using RLS as a rallying-point for other agents. Perhaps the British
were tricking him in their turn! Did they know that Lauwers
was transmitting under control, and were now setting a trap for
Giskes? It was strange that these disquieting questions had occurred to both Lauwers and Giskes.

Here was a fresh problem and fresh hopes, bringing fresh agi-
tation. Schreieder would have to act with the utmost speed. The
Abwehr chief wanted to have all control. Nothing and nobody
else mattered. He wanted all the other Lauwers to be chained to
their transmitters. All the other radio operators hidden about
Holland, as well as those dropped in the future, must *all* be captured and assembled in the dungeons of *Abwehr 111/F*.

Canaris's disciple wanted to impress his master. He also wanted to show the military strategists that his secret war, which they all despised, was worth quite as much as any campaign fought in the mud, sand or snow.

It was as much as Major Giskes could do not to shout there and then 'Arrest the lot!' Instead, he turned to Lauwers and said: 'The tobacconist at The Hague? Which tobacconist's is that, Lieutenant Lauwers?'

'I don't know,' said Lauwers.

Giskes did not pursue the matter. It might well be that Lauwers did not know; the message was not for him, he merely had to pass it on to Takonis. Besides, it was not Giskes's concern. It was Schreieder's job, with his pack of informers, his black-uniformed policemen and blue-uniformed policemen (the Duch), to track down 'Pijl' and bring him in so that he, too, could transmit under German control. Giskes would not have had a hand in the police side of the operation at any price. Schreieder, on the other hand, who modestly styled himself a criminologist, loved a manhunt. He ought to be able to lay hands on 'Pijl' (Arrow) within a week.

Giskes was thinking aloud. Lauwers thus learned (Giskes saw no reason to hide it from him) that another of his comrades would soon be captured. It seemed to Lauwers that his head was just an anvil which the major beat while smiling and chatting. How would it all end? Why, oh why would the British not understand? It was now a month to the day, to the very hour, since he had sent his first message.

In spite of the Spring weather, the nights were still cold. Lauwers shivered in the unheated car which took him back to Haaren. He had glanced at himself in the driving mirror and seen a few white hairs on his temples. Even if the firing squad were delayed, he would soon die of worry or go out of his mind from turning over the same questions.

Takonis, no longer chained but still in solitary confinement, was little better. In fact, it was worse with him. He had soon concluded that it was better not to try to understand. He was a prisoner, and perhaps that was best for all concerned. Takonis had not tried to work out the reasons. He had refused to talk right from the start, and since then he had slowly sunk into a kind of torpor; nothing seemed to affect him any more. He sat all day slumped against the wall with his legs tucked under him. He refused to take exercise, but not food; a hunger-strike would have drawn attention to him. All he wanted was to sink silently into oblivion, unnoticed, to merge slowly into the saltpetre on the walls of the prison.

Schreieder had been notified within an hour of the message being received – not by Giskes (the major would on no account beg the help of the *Kriminalrat*) but by Heinrichs, who had hurried to the Binnenhoff and found Schreieder about to leave. Heinrichs explained his errand.

'The tobacconist's at The Hague ... ?' Which tobacconist's? There were at least three hundred. He, Schreieder, could not be expected to mobilise an army just for one agent. He sat down at his desk again, lit the green-shaded lamp and held his head in his hands. Heinrichs, standing to attention a few paces away, watched him concentrating. Schreieder was a small man endowed with great strength and powers. When the time came to act, he became a relentless machine, a miniature version of the Rauter machine. Not a single part was missing. In 1938, he had been involved in 'settling the Jewish problem' in the Sudeten, and was seen to be a cold-eyed monster, splendidly organised, insensitive and inhuman. And now, as he took his hands from his face, Heinrichs saw the change that had come over it. He said it was too late to go to Haaren that evening, but he would go in the morning.

He was there by seven, and a jailer took him to Takonis's cell and opened the door wide. A week before, Takonis would have spat in Schreieder's face as he had in Giskes's. But 'long Thijs' was a changed man, hunched against the wall with a fixed smile on his face. He slowly bowed his head and joined his hands together like a Hindu priest. Schreieder stood there before him, legs apart and arms folded. Formerly, Takonis had been a hero whose name was mentioned with great respect by other prisoners. Now he was as nothing, inert. He had stopped wondering who had betrayed him; he had cut himself off.

He raised his head as slowly as he had lowered it. 'Takonis!' Schreieder's harsh voice rapped out. 'Give me Pijl's address! At once! The address of the tobacconist's!'

He gave it. But not Takonis, only the shadow of the man.

Schreieder was back in his office by midday. Van der Waals was 'working' at Utrecht. He had changed a great deal in a year. On

Schreieder's order, he had got into the habit of washing himself and dressing better, and with some taste. It must be said that he now had the means. In the year he had betrayed a hundred agents and Resistance members to Schreieder! A bag of ten men was worth, on average, three thousand guilders, plus expenses and in addition to his salary. Not bad at all. He had a steady job for the first time in his life. In his rare moments of leisure he was generous to the girls he met along by the canals, pressing cheap jewellery upon them. He drank a little, but very little, as alcohol did not agree with him. His main concern was to put money by for after the war, so that he could buy the Steinway piano of his dreams and the equipment he needed for his research work. With this in view, he worked very hard, much harder than Ridderhoff, and more intelligently.

He had perfected his technique. His method was to work his way into a Resistance group by claiming to be an agent from London. The Dutch patriots were invariably suspicious; they distrusted his volubility, and his face hardly inspired confidence. When they told him so, he shrugged his shoulders and went away, but he was soon brought back, as a man who already knew so much could not be allowed to go free. Whereupon he sulked for an hour or so, then relented and *forgave* them. He even agreed to provide proof; he mentioned names, decoded messages sent over Radio Oranje for agents whose capture by Schreieder was not known to the Resistance.

However, he had still not gained their complete confidence; he was put to the test, given a rendezvous for the following day. At this second meeting, Van der Waals spoke of an escape route, of an expected parachute drop, and said that he carried definite orders from the Gerbrandy government. The patriots became more confident, and Van der Waals's notebook bulged with names and addresses. Then one day he got them all to meet in the entrance-hall of some hotel in Breda or Apeldoorn, and Schreieder arrived on the scene with his men. Antonius was arrested with the others, even putting up a vigorous resistance and playing his part magnificently right to the end.

In this way he sent many members of the underground to their deaths, and without showing the slightest emotion (he did say later that he sometimes cried when he reached home in the evening). For a little money, he killed by proxy many brave but inexperienced men, good folk who worked as solicitors' clerks, grocers or labourers, who had clear blue eyes, knew nothing about espionage, sabotage or secret warfare in general; men whose courage did not falter and who nearly all died without talking, without knowing who had betrayed them or why. Van der Waals would not have deceived professional Intelligence agents for a moment, as he well knew. In fact, he was terrified of coming up against *real* British agents.

Schreieder was not the least bit impatient at midday on 29 April. He knew that Antonius (as he paternally called him) would ring him at one o'clock, as he did every day, to make his report and to ask for instructions in his thin, almost inaudible voice. Van der Waals duly rang, but before he could get in a word, Schreieder said: 'Return at once. I'll be waiting for you at the Binnenhoff.'

Van der Waals was probably very worried and anxious during the short journey from Utrecht to The Hague. What urgent reason could have caused the *Kriminalrat* to order him to drop the matter in hand (he had just infiltrated into a small group of hotheaded youngsters – Communists)? Schreieder had not sounded very pleased – perhaps he had slipped up somewhere. Antonius hated scenes, shouting and argument.

He was breathless when he entered Schreieder's office. He had decided to ward off the *Kriminalrat*'s shouts by pleading fatigue. It was unnecessary, for the latter was all smiles.

'Sit down,' he said 'and listen to me.' He tried to fix Van der Waals with his eyes. 'Look up! That's better. Now then, listen to me. I'm going to give you a job that might well be the most important in your whole career.'

Van der Waals did not like the sound of that. Schreieder was undoubtedly going to pit him against real agents.

Agents are like insects which have legs and a hard casing, antennae and an acute sense of danger but lack eyes and ears. The SOE training had improved the agents' reflexes and judgment, given them a sixth sense when trailed in the street, when suddenly attacked and when stopped by cars. And they usually slipped through the net.

But when a man like Van der Waals stepped into the tobacconist's, raised his hat, asked the assistant if he had any 'Ritter' cigars and went on to say that he wished to speak to Pijl, the agent Akki's face lit up with a smile; he was only too pleased at meeting another patriot and suspected nothing.

'Come with me,' he said, slipping on a coat.

He led the way down a street next to the Staatsport railway station and turned into the café. There was a red glow from the lighting inside, like pre-war days, and a smell of real gin floated about. Akki tapped Van der Waals's hand—he was not to worry, Pijl would soon arrive. Some Resistance members met here every afternoon at four o'clock.

Pijl came in, a man with a fervent look like Takonis. He frowned when he saw the stranger. But Akki introduced him as 'Van Lob', (the name Van der Waals had given), 'an agent come from London to coordinate our activities'. Pijl was still suspicious. Where had Akki met this person? He had not met him. Van Lob had come to the shop on behalf of 'long Thijs', who was active in the north, in the Drente, and could not come himself.

By giving this story, Van der Waals had put his life in the balance. It was an even chance whether Pijl knew that Takonis had been captured. There was a short silence. Then Pijl suddenly asked, 'What's he like – Thijs?'

Van der Waals had it pat. 'He's tall and dark, never says very much. Probably a half-caste.'

'And what did he tell you?'

'He told me to come and help you. That's all. It's an order from London.'

Luck was with Van der Waals. In the first place, Akki and Pijl did not know that Takonis had been wasting away in prison for a month, and secondly Akki's radio operator had been killed when landing three weeks before, and Pijl's transmitter had been smashed to pieces when he had been dropped. Since then, both men had been wandering round Holland trying to find a way of contacting with London. They badly needed an experienced radio operator. Six weeks earlier, Pijl had met Takonis, who had promised to do what he could, but then vanished.

However, there were hopes, now that Van Lob had turned up. Pijl did not like the look of the man very much, but in present circumstances one could not be fussy about the appearance of agents one met. Anyway, an ugly face was nothing to go by. And Thijs must have had a good reason for sending this Van Lob.

79

Antonius saw that he had pulled it off. So he sat talking with the two men, feeling compelled to keep up the act. He chatted away, calling Pijl familiarly 'old chap'. Schreieder had warned him a dozen times about behaving like some commercial traveller when out on a job like this. But it was all to no avail. Schreieder did not realise that his Antonius felt an urgent need to play the fool after being frightened to death. This was his way of recovering his poise. It was a failing which would cost him dear one day.

They parted after about an hour, having arranged to meet at the same place the following day. Neither Pijl nor his friend felt much confidence in Van Lob, but they saw no reason to suspect him either. This was typically amateurish.

Van der Waals turned up his coat-collar as he left the café, glanced furtively to right and left, then hurried off, head bent against the stinging April rain. Akki and Pijl did not trail him, which was a serious mistake on their part. They would have seen him make his way through the narrow twisting streets around the Staatsport station, then jump on a crowded tram. The conductor wanted him to get off again, but Van der Waal produced a red-and-black striped card in a mica case. Five minutes later, he walked into the Binnenhoff. If only Akki or Pijl had followed him!

Twenty-four hours later, Akki and Pijl were again sitting in the red-lit café. They both ordered gin. Pijl said that he wished he had questioned Van Lob more thoroughly. 'I ought to have insisted that he brought Thijs with him today.' Akki pointed out that they had already lost a lot of time. Besides, the man had proved that he knew Thijs; he had described him, and had given the code used by London. Akki reassured his friend – 'the Arrow' had found the bow he needed. They ordered another gin.

They never drank it. Seven men all wearing grey-blue raincoats surged into the café. One brandished a revolver, and motioned to everybody to put up their hands. Akki and Pijl made a move towards the back room, but the seven men were on them at once, bound and gagged them and dragged them outside. As he left the café, Schreieder told the barman that he could lower his hands.

That was just one stage of the round-up. The radio detection vans had picked up signals from a clandestine transmitter; while this was still functioning, the success of Operation North Pole was in the balance.

Akki and Pijl were given the full Gestapo treatment. Inspector Bayer and May took turns at putting the pressure on as they would have squeezed a lemon dry, hoping that more names, addresses and meeting-places could be forced from between the bruised and swollen lips of the two hapless agents.

Hermann Giskes had himself gone to fetch Lauwers from Haaren prison. At six o'clock on the evening of 29 April 1942, Hubertus was again seated before his transmitter. No explanation was given to him, and he knew nothing of the happenings on the previous day. Giskes handed him a sheet of paper with the day's message for London written on it: 'Thijs has contacted Pijl.'

'Is that all?' he asked.

'It's quite enough,' said Giskes.

Lauwers had always had his role explained to him; this was the first time he had been left in the dark. He realised that something big was in the offing, that other agents were about to be captured, but he did not know when, where or how. Nor did he know who were the men soon to be dropped. He was just a tool.

By now, he could not bear to look at his set and he loathed the table it stood on. Giskes's Turkish cigarettes made him feel sick. As for Heinrichs – tall, black-uniformed, pink-complexioned, benevolent – he would gladly have strangled him. He wished that the underground room where he worked, surrounded by soldiers in field-green uniform, would cave in and bury everybody, himself included.

However, Lauwers did not show his reluctance. He made contact with London and sent the short message, ending with 'Stip' instead of 'Stop', and not. . . . This reflex had supplanted the other, the one he had acquired during his training. He did it purely for his own satisfaction, for no one, either in London or at The Hague, took any notice of it. In fact, as he looked up he saw that Heinrichs had not put his headphones on. For the first time, Heinrichs was not troubling to check what he was sending. Heinrichs trusted him! Lauwers felt humiliated.

It was about then, or perhaps a little earlier, that Akki broke down under torture and told May – or Bayer – that other agents and Resistance members met daily in the café of the Terminus Hotel at Utrecht. These members of the underground found their isolation hard to bear and met in the busiest public place in the town. There they made a little group of solemn young men, pooling their information. One of them, who had been a Signals officer in the Dutch Army, had a transmitter and sent the information to London. He was the man whom Giskes so badly needed. Neither Akki nor Pijl had ever met him. They did not know his name, only that he existed. While they were being taken back to their cells, covered in blood and barely conscious, broken in mind and body, the final stage of the round-up was being prepared.

Akki cannot be considered a traitor. He had talked, admittedly. But his head was bursting from the blows; they had broken his teeth one by one, they had crushed his penis with their boots, they had stuck white-hot needles under his finger-nails. He had been humiliated as well as tortured. Only one misfortune evaded him – not to die or even faint under the first blows. When he did talk, he had ceased to be a man, what is usually meant by a man. He was just a bundle of bones and muscles and nerves on which pain could still be inflicted. They had not limited themselves to torturing and humiliating him. They had told him that all his comrades had been captured and that he had been betrayed by London. As proof, there was the fact that Lauwers – yes, Lauwers, that great patriot – had been working for the Germans for the past month. Lauwers had been the first to realise that the British abandoned their Dutch agents as soon as they set foot in Holland. It was all a diabolical masquerade, typically English. These feeble arguments might not have had a direct effect but had all contributed to break down Akki and Pijl. No one can say: 'In their place, I'd never have talked.'

At five in the afternoon of 30 April, while Akki and Pijl were trying to find sleep in their cells, despite their injuries, a squad of Dutch and German policemen in civilian clothes stepped through the main entrance of the Terminus Hotel at Utrecht. They spread out over the large, well-appointed café where a few retired, prosperous men and plump elderly ladies with large hats were having tea – the kind of people whose way of life remains undisturbed even by war and enemy occupation. The police soon saw the little group they were looking for in this haven of peace – the four young men had kept their overcoats on and had even turned their collars up, making themselves more conspicuous. The two agents, Ras and Kloos, and the two Resistance members were handcuffed before they knew what was happening.

They were hustled out, shouting and struggling like children being bundled out of a park. They still did not realise that these jovial fellows (Dutchmen!) who had pounced on them were arresting them for the Germans, more precisely for the Gestapo. ('I thought at first that they were playing a joke on us,' Ras said later.)

There was a slight stir among the onlookers, but a few minutes later they were again absorbed in their crosswords and gossip. It could only have been some student rag (Utrecht is a university town), nothing that really mattered. And peace, ruffled for a moment, returned to the Terminus Hotel.

Ras was a meticulous young man who left nothing to chance. He had a big black notebook in which he wrote down, in a neat, legible hand, everything he learned, heard or even suspected. Schreieder found a clear lead in it. Ras had written that he had a rendezvous in Laren with a man calling himself Jeffers. He had even written down the man's real name, Jacob Jordaan; and opposite it had put 'radio operator'.

It was a despondent Van der Waals who took the train to Laren. He was calling himself Van Dijk this time. He was alone, he had never been to Laren and no one there knew him. Still, he was scared. The recent arrests had probably put the various Resistance groups very much on the alert. Whenever he felt himself out on a limb, without the immediate support of the huge Gestapo machine, Van der Waals began to lose confidence.

So when he arrived at Laren, he cheated. Instead of going to the address which had been given him, he went into a café, sat down and called for a glass of *schnaps* and the telephone directory. Heartened by the drink, he flicked over the pages of the directory, looking for Mevrouw X (Jordaan's landlady). It was so much simpler and – he dared not admit to himself – safer to ring up first. He would say that he was a friend of Pijl, of Takonis, Ras, Kloos – everybody's friend. On the telephone, out of reach, he forgot his fears and was therefore more convincing. Everything impelled him to take this course. It might be a cowardly way out, but he had never pretended to be a hero. He went to the call box and dialled the number. He heard it ringing, and almost at once a man replied.

Van Dijk introduced himself. There was no tremor in his voice

– nor in Jordaan's; it sounded like that of a decisive young man, a very young man. He said 'Yes, yes, good, agreed,' when Antonius proposed that they should meet outside a certain telephone kiosk at Rotterdam on 3 May. He did not ask why the meeting had to be in Rotterdam. This meek agreement from a responsible person like Jordaan was odd. And why had he not asked for the password? Van der Waal's suspicious mind and his intelligence were on a par with his physical fears. When he left the kiosk he was feeling most uneasy; he did not like the sound of Jordaan's docile acceptance of his proposal. He paid for his *schnaps*, turned up his coat-collar and went out of the café like a fox leaving its earth. But there was no one waiting for him; Laren was completely unaware of his presence. In its mournful streets, people were passing each other unseeingly, wrapped up in their own affairs.

Rotterdam, that was fine, Antonius need not go to the rendezvous himself. Schreieder could send his police. If it was a trap, if Jordaan had some Resistance men waiting round the corner of the square, ready to open fire, then the Gestapo would be able to cope with the situation. But not Antonius.

There was a thick sea-mist seeping into Rotterdam on the morning of 3 May, creeping through the ruins and the crumbling buildings. Here and there a few families had rigged up shelters among the bombed houses with planks and tarpaulins. Otherwise, the population of the bombed area had moved out to the northern suburbs of the city.

It was still cold at ten-thirty. Van der Waals, forced by the *Kriminalrat* to come to the rendezvous, was wearing a thick muffler. He walked across the deserted square with his hands in his pockets. He could just see the yellow kiosk when he got to within fifty yards of it, but the mist prevented him from telling whether anyone was standing inside. He wondered why Schreieder had made him come. 'You're indispensable. You'll be the bait,' was all that the Gestapo chief had said to him. At the moment, Van der Waals did not know whether he was alone or whether Schreieder had placed men round the square. If so, there was no sign of them. He walked on towards the yellow kiosk. Against Schreieder's strict orders, he had brought a heavy revolver with him, and it was making a bulge in his right trouser pocket. But he knew he was no shot, especially on the draw. And he had no illusions about himself – at the first sign of danger, instead of pulling out his revolver he would take to his heels.

He walked steadily on, and when he was about ten yards from the kiosk there came a sudden break in the mist, and he saw there was someone inside the kiosk. A fair-haired youngster was waiting for Van Dijk to arrive: he had lifted the receiver, to look natural, and was nodding slowly to give the impression that he was listening to someone at the other end. He was just as Van der Waals had imagined him from his voice – a mere child, an infant whom Van der Waals was about to send to his death.

Antonius turned away. He had caught only a glimpse of Jordaan, but for the first time it occurred to him that he was about to commit a crime. Jordaan – if it was indeed him – could only be a student playing at war in between lessons. But was this youngster really Jordaan? Van der Waals turned back again and walked straight towards the kiosk. The lad looked at him and at once put back the receiver. He recognised him (Antonius had said he would wear a red muffler), left the kiosk and hurried smilingly to meet him. Antonius moved away.

But it was no good, it was too late. The police, conjured out of the mist and the ruins, pounced on Jordaan at once.

'Why are you doing this?' cried Jordaan.

He did not know that Major Giskes was reckoning on him to extend and strengthen the *England Spiel*.

7

The Trap

Jordaan was no youngster – he was twenty-four years of age. He was no longer a student either, and he had been in the Dutch Navy before volunteering for SOE. He was not working on his own. His SOE training had made him a very good radio operator and he had been dropped on 10 March 1942 at the same time as the two saboteurs, Kloos and Ras.

It had been thought that his baby face and well-combed fair hair, his look of a spoilt lad of good family and his refined speech, articulating his words through milky-white teeth, would allay suspicion. And so they had. At Laren, where everyone spied on his neighbour, this handsome, tidy young man had been set up as an example to others. But Akki, Pijl, Ras and Kloos had each made slight admissions, thinking they were of no importance, and so had put the Gestapo on Jordaan's tail.

He was crying now. His captors still thought they had arrested a mere child, and a few of them even seemed embarrassed. Schreieder wondered if this really was Jeffers, alias Jordaan, but Van der Waals said he was sure of it. Jordaan had been left alone in a cell, no one had questioned him or knocked him about. But he was in a state of collapse, half-dead with shame, wondering who had betrayed him and convinced that he would be shot.

Takonis the just, a man born to be a dumb martyr, had ended by cracking up. So it would not be long, thought Giskes, before this 'novice' at secret warfare was transmitting under his control alongside Lauwers. Giskes would soon hold a few more cards – without moving from his chair, he would make a success of the most fantastic *Funkspiel* in the history of counter-intelligence, and all due to himself.

By 4 May 1942, Hermann Giskes thought he had laid a perfect trap for the British. He no longer wondered about the astonishing way in which the enemy swallowed messages dictated by himself. Why should he? The British continued to drop weapons, and agents too. They would surely not send technicians, officers, to their death just to make the Germans think they had been duped, it was unthinkable. Hermann Giskes had every confidence. More agents were going to come floating down – the British had promised they would.

When Jordaan woke up in his cell the following morning, 5 May, he tried to wipe a hand across his face but found that his left wrist had been chained to the central-heating pipe. Out in the corridor, a guard with a submachine-gun slung from the shoulder was looking at him a little pityingly.

'I don't understand,' Jordaan groaned at him. 'I haven't hurt anyone.'

The guard (a young recruit, thin and gloomy, whose SS badges seemed laughable) merely shrugged his shoulders. There was only one way out for Jordaan – to play the innocent right to the end. He might convince them that they had made a mistake and arrested the wrong person. With a little luck, by weeping copiously or staying dignified and aloof, he might get away with it. He could think only of death awaiting him, unaware that a certain Major Giskes needed him very much alive. But he was soon to find out.

The *Abwehr* took him over from the Gestapo. It was about ten o'clock that morning when the fair-haired boy found himself face to face with the bulky major. The more important documents found by Van der Waals were spread out on the table, before an attentive gathering of *Abwehr* clerks and officers. Giskes had arranged them in an orderly manner, as though showing off a masterly hand of cards. Jordaan saw his address book open at the page on which he had written his code-name, 'Trumpet'. Next to it was a thick exercise book with 'Chemistry' written in round letters on the cover. He had used this for copying and dating all the messages that he transmitted to London! It was an amazing collection of clandestine documents – letters, addresses of 'safe' houses and outlines of plans. His transmitter was there too, a clean, shiny black set standing on an adjacent table. Heinrichs was checking it over; it seemed almost new, as if fresh from the factory. Jordaan had probably looked after it very carefully.

When Jordaan gave a quick glance round the room he saw there was one civilian among the military, a man of indeterminate age and nationality. He was staring at Jordaan. His drawn features and the dark rings under his eyes showed that he had been in prison or living down a mine for some time. His eyes suddenly began blinking rapidly, as if he had just stepped into strong sunlight.

'Who are you?' said Lauwers.

Jordaan gave his name.

'You're also called Jeffers,' stated Giskes. He took him by the arm and led him up to the table with the documents. 'Look – it's all there. We don't need to question you. Here's your complete confession!'

Jordaan refused the cigarette that the major offered him. Then Giskes made the same liittle speech, though more concisely, that he had served up to Lauwers the day after his arrest. Giskes added that Lauwers, a brilliant officer, here in the room with them, had agreed two months ago to cooperate with him, in order to end this stupid, fratricidal struggle.

Jordaan looked more closely at Lauwers. He saw an apparently normal man, neither weaker nor braver than the average. Weariness had destroyed what character and strength there had been in the face, but one could still see that in the past, probably fairly recently, Lauwers had been somebody respectable. He was a little older than Jordaan.

Giskes left the two together for a moment or so, neither spoke, they just studied the other's face. Then the major took Jordaan by the arm again and continued working on him.

'Lieutenant Lauwers is not the only member of your organisation who has agreed to work for us.' (Jordaan was still wondering, in his numb mind, what the major was leading up to.) 'Other agents, all the agents we've captured, have agreed! That, incidentally, is why they are still alive.' Giskes stopped and let this sink in, then drove in the final wedge.

'Mr Jordaan, you were dropped by parachute on 10 March at the same time as the saboteur Ras, in the region of Holten. Is that correct?' Jordaan nodded, then lowered his head like a little boy who had been found out. 'Good. On the same date, as you must know, two other SOE agents were dropped – Akki, whose real name is Andringa, and his radio operator, Maartens. The latter

88

fractured his skull on landing. Correct? And on 19 April, the agent De Haas, nicknamed Pijl, was landed by motorboat somewhere near Katwijk. Pijl brought with him a radio-telephone device which enabled him to communicate with other agents. That is how he got in touch with you. He was supposed to meet you very soon. That is all quite true, isn't it?'

'Yes,' muttered Jordaan.

It was all quite true, terribly true. In twenty-four hours as a prisoner, Jordaan had learned more about the art of secret warfare than in six months' training in England. He had thought he was quite safe, an invisible spy with a perfect cover, but he might well have been working in the open. He had trusted the first person to contact him – Van der Waals. He had always believed that the men he was in touch with, whom he sometimes met, were exceptional people. But they had all fallen into enemy hands, just like him and even before him.

Giskes ended his summary with a few telling statements, turning the knife in Jordaan's wounds.

'I also know that the missions given to agents had various code names. Yours was "Lettuce", otherwise called the "Trumpet" plan. Andringa's mission had the code-name "Turnip". The mission of Kloos and Sebes was called "Leek". All these agents have been captured. They have all agreed to work with me.' Giskes said 'with me' on purpose, so that Jordaan should see that it was not a question of cooperating with the black-uniformed men but with officers of good breeding and education.

Jordaan looked at Lauwers, then back at Giskes and his men. There was nothing sinister about the atmosphere and surroundings. They were a thousand miles from the filthy war being waged above. This underground room in the *Abwehr* Citadel was well heated. The smell of Turkish cigarettes and real coffee was comforting.

But it must be a trap, the most insidious set by Major Giskes.

'I'm no traitor!' Jordaan cried. 'I'll never work with you!'

It was the night of 29 May 1942, and in a field near Steenwijk everyone was ready and waiting. The two SOE agents, Parlevliet and Van Steen (the 'Beetroot' mission), jumped from the plane. There was no wind, and the two parachutes floated slowly down towards the 'reception committee'.

The men on the ground saw the two land a few yards from a hedge, and waited for them to approach. There were hearty greetings. Parlevliet and Van Steen spoke of their mission, which was to instal an infra-red device to communicate with Allied warships cruising off the Dutch coast. They were also the bearers of a plan to sabotage German naval radar stations. They were happy to be talking to friends in Holland, after their isolation during the few days before their departure from England. The friends in question listened with great interest, nodding gravely. Then, when they heard everything, including the code names of Van Steen and Parlevliet, they handcuffed the two young men. Schreieder emerged from a thicket while the two were still struggling and cursing at the traitors who had arrested them.

On 22 June, near Holten, at about the same time of night, two more agents came floating down. Their names were Rietschoten and Buizer, and their mission ('Parsnip') was to organise the Dutch Resistance. They were received as their predecessors had been at Steenwijk.

Still more agents were dropped, quite regularly. Two a week, on average. Giskes's dream had come true. He had five lines of communication with London. He had the codes, if not all the security checks. In a matter of weeks, his trap had taken shape and been extended. It was difficult to see what could impede the working. Before the year was out, the Resistance in Holland would have been strangled, eliminated.

One day in April 1942, Churchill presided over a meeting of a few of his ministers. His thoughts seemed much less occupied with Europe, now that Allied strength was building up in North Africa. He was heard to say that 'the war will be decided in Africa and in Russia, and nowhere else'. Eden had reported to him periodically on the progress or otherwise of Resistance activities in Europe. But he had scarcely listened, as if no longer convinced of the value in the complex, secret organisation which was his brainchild.

However, on this occasion he informed his closest colleagues of his intention to probe in strength at the German defences along the French Channel coast. The purpose was twofold. In the first place, despite Intelligence reports, there was no precise information as to the number and strength of the German divisions stationed on or near the coast. Secondly, Stalin was demanding the opening of a Second Front. By attempting a landing on the French coast, the British would be showing their willingness but also, since the attempt seemed bound to fail, that they were not yet strong enough to make a successful invasion.

In other words, in April 1942, plans were already being made for the raid on Dieppe. . . .

8

The Awakening

Lauwers was no longer the only radio operator being notified of the impending arrival of more of his comrades. Somewhere in The Hague, 'Pijl' (De Haas) was transmitting under Giskes's control. And then there was Jordaan. He had passed from secrecy to sham treachery – from one world to another – without much difficulty, without losing any sleep. Lauwers had told him that the Germans could be tricked, and Jordaan had disclosed a false security check too. They worked side by side, either in the underground room at *Abwehr* headquarters or at the seaside villa. There was only Heinrichs, and sometimes Huntemann, to keep watch on them. They were allowed to talk between themselves, and took full advantage of it.

'Even if it does no good, even if the British don't give a damn, we must carry on with it,' said Lauwers. 'They haven't *read* that I'm working under German control, so I'll make it plainer for them. Between the two of us, that should be easier to do.'

Heinrichs was looking at these two secret agents of Free Holland – Jordaan, and Lauwers who might have been some humble clerk. They were not at all what he had imagined professional spies to be like. But then they were not professionals. What could have made the British Command send such boobies, who could be turned with just a blow or a threat, he wondered? They had been thrown into a fight beyond their capacity. Heinrichs was becoming a little sorry for them. His superiors were rarely present at transmissions (Gieskes had better things to do, and Schreieder did not have right of entry to *Abwehr* headquarters), and Heinrichs was getting into the habit of chatting with the two while waiting for the scheduled time.

Jordaan was still holding aloof, but Lauwers was quite ready to discuss the war, Germany and the Dutch, in general terms. Heinrichs thought that Lauwers expressed his ideas well. He was the sort of thoughtful, sensible man with whom, had it not been for the war, Heinrichs would willingly have made friends. He frequently relaxed his watch on the two, who transmitted one after the other but coded their messages together. He sometimes put down his headphones while one or the other was transmitting.

Lauwers seized the opportunity to change a letter or a figure in his message; he jumbled up two letters, a word, several words. Jordaan did the same, but blushed while doing it, which could have given him away. Jordaan was a much better radio operator than Lauwers, but could not control his emotions. So it was Lauwers who sent the distress signal, the great warning, while Jordaan kept an eye on the German officer's reactions.

It happened on 4 June 1942.

Lauwers was huddled over his set. He had taken off his jacket (the weather was very close, with frequent thunderstorms, and the heat had even got into the big underground radio room). Jordaan was sitting next to him, coding the messages to be sent to London. They had been able to decide on their plan while in prison, communicating over the pipes in Morse and having a few words together during the daily exercise hour.

It was four in the afternoon. Heinrichs looked enviously at his two prisoners. They were in their shirt-sleeves, but he could not take off his uniform jacket. Perspiration ran down his face, his hands were sticky, and the headphones were like two little hot water-bottles pressed against his ears, making listening almost unbearable.

Lauwers had got the frequency – a continuous low whistling indicated that London was waiting to receive him. He started transmitting. He had a few items of information to send, and a reply to an important question – 'Are you ready to receive two agents at the end of June?' The reply was simply 'yes'.

Lauwers repeated his call-sign three times, as usual. He looked at Jordaan, who glanced at Heinrichs. The German had undone the two top buttons of his uniform. He was looking down at the sheet of squared paper which had a copy of the message written on it. Although suffering from the heat, he was still vigilant.

Lauwers began tapping out the message. 'Anti-aircraft batteries around Rotterdam been increased.' (Quite true, but London knew it already; it would give an authentic touch to the rest.) 'Tank regiment moving up to the Belgian frontier.' (Probably true, but nobody would go and check it.) Jordaan gave three little taps on the table – the pre-arranged signal.

Heinrichs had not been able to stand it any longer. He had slipped off the headphones and was poking his left forefinger into his ear.

Without even glancing at the German, Lauwers tapped out:
'No. 36. No. 36. 18 GR. 18 GR. 18 GR. 18. 34. 512. 34. 512. ETKGO. ETKGO. NSPNO. NSPNO.'
'CAUGHT. CAUGHT.' he had sent in English.
'Lauwers! What have you just sent?'

Jordaan was so scared that he had been watching Lauwers instead of Heinrichs, and had not seen the German put his headphones on again. Heinrichs had picked up 'C-A-U-G-H-T' and realised at once that these letters were not in the text of the message. In a split second he ceased to be the chatty, conciliatory, understanding Heinrichs (all astonishing in a SS officer). The savage watchdog in him barked at Lauwers. And Jordaan hung his head like a naughty boy.

'Have you gone crazy, Lauwers! What are you up to?'

Heinrichs attitude was very threatening. But Lauwers and Jordaan both saw that he had not heard enough to understand what was really going on. Lauwers had been careful to conceal his cry of distress in among a number of letters and figures. Heinrichs had not *read* the English word. He thought it was due to tiredness on Lauwer's part. He was roused, but not suspicious.

'Do it again, Lauwers. You've made a mess of it!'

Lauwers began again – his call-sign, then the first sentence of the message. Heinrichs was following each letter, his finger on the sheet of squared paper. What did Lauwers have to lose? Death would come a little sooner, that was all. He reached the point where he had sent 'caught' instead of 'crag', and he did the same thing again, slowly this time, so that there should be no mistake – so that the British should clearly understand at last.

There were more yells from Heinrichs. But he still suspected nothing. He was telling Lauwers to begin yet again when London started sending in sharp, clear Morse. The message was quite short: 'Not understood please repeat.'

'You see?' Heinrichs exulted. 'You see? They haven't understood it! What's come over you, Lauwers?'

He had calmed down, his slight suspicion now dispelled.

Lauwers began again. He was thinking that if he did not go
through with it today, he never would. He would remain in his
rut, in his black hole, and no one would ever get him out of it.
He purposely fumbled over sending the first part of the message,
jumbled a letter or two and looked at Heinrichs apologetically,
gestured that he was tired and ought to give up. Heinrichs could
understand that, Lauwers was bound to lose control of his nerves
now and again, after transmitting under pressure for so long. Each
time Lauwers made a mistake, he corrected it at once. Heinrichs
stamped his foot impatiently, but did not insist on Lauwers starting again at the beginning. And so for the fourth time, Lauwers
sent 'caught' instead of 'crag'. He corrected it at once, but the
word had gone out, sent slowly and distinctly.

Four times, Lauwers had sent a clear warning to the British.

Four times, he had told them he was captured.

Four times, he had clearly explained that they must not drop
any more agents, that the farce had gone on long enough. Lauwers
ended his message and the three sat waiting for the reply from
London. It was a long time coming. A quarter of an hour went
by, during which Heinrichs lectured Lauwers, telling him that
he should work better than that. He was tired, obviously, but he
must try to overcome it. Lauwers and Jordaan nodded in
agreement.

When the whistling sound came at last, Lauwers and Heinrichs
each clamped his headphones to his ears. There was some slight
crackling for a moment or two, then the signal in Morse was heard
clear and distinct. The British operator repeated his message three
times. It was extremely brief. Three times he sent:

'Message understood.'

9

The Radio Game

It was high time they understood. At that very moment, SOE was about to launch its biggest operation, 'Plan Holland'. This could be summed up in one word—sabotage, sabotage, and more sabotage. In a matter of weeks, an army was to be raised in the shadows to paralyse German Army movements in Holland.

It was time they understood. This 'Secret Army' was to be organised by a man of great prestige and valour, who had been specially trained and briefed in England – George Louis Jambroes who before the war was Professor of Physics at Utrecht University. Jambroes had escaped to England in December 1941. At the Patriotic School, the selection board had wanted him to assist British scientists who were working on the development of radar. But Jambroes had refused and volunteered for 'special work' instead.

He had great renown as a scientist (the Germans had offered him enormous sums to work for them), so the Baker Street men had chosen him to represent the spirit of Resistance. They held many conferences to brief him for his mission. Most important, he was told, 'Holland is to be divided into seventeen military districts. You will be sent ten instructors and ten radio operators who will train and organise the Resistance groups under your orders. Your close collaborators will be Vermeulen and Vorrink. These two are now the leaders of Resistance activities in Holland. More detailed instructions will be sent to you after your arrival in Holland.'

Shortly before midnight on 25 June 1942, a Halifax bomber was about to take off from a RAF aerodrome in south-east England. The night was clear, 'good weather for the bombers', as people in the big towns used to say with apprehension. The Halifax carried no bombs. In addition to the crew, there were just two men squatting in the bomb bay with their arms folded over their parachutes. The aircraft soon gained height, and the ears of the two men became affected. They put on their leather helmets, hoping to relieve the buzzing in their heads, and drew the straps tight under their chins.

The weather over the North Sea was bad, and as the Halifax crossed the Belgian coast it was shaken by flak. The two passengers were thrown about: both were sick, and the horrid thought came to them that they might die while unprepared. But suddenly there was quiet – the plane seemed to be flying through cotton-wool. It began to lose height, and fifteen minutes later one of the crew opened the hatch. What followed was like a nightmare. There was no noise in the fuselage, just a purple light which would change to red when the moment came to jump. One of the men sat on the edge of the hatch with his legs dangling in space. The red light came on, and he vanished. The other took his place – the red light, and he jumped.

They landed within a hundred yards of each other, more softly than when making practice jumps; the Dutch soil is very light. They peeled off their parachutes and then saw some men running towards them with outstretched arms.

'God save the Queen!' they cried.

'God save Holland!'

The two were given hot coffee, behind a clump of trees. They were taken by the arm. It was an emotional moment, the meeting with these men, so different from themselves, who had been fighting in the shadows for the same cause for nearly two years. It was understandable that they should grip the arms of the two delegates from the free world so tightly.

A small man came forward and asked, 'What's your name?'

This sudden curtness was very odd. And the plump little man's accent was strange.

'Bukkens,' said the younger of the two parachutists.

'And yours?'

The other did not answer at once. He looked at the faces around him. Except for the plump little man, they all looked agreeable enough.

'My name is Jambroes,' he said.

Perhaps Giskes and his associates were right when they asserted that the British were just apprentices, and had set up an organisation which they were not capable of controlling properly. Or perhaps Baatsen, Van Steen and the other prisoners were right when they declared: 'There's a traitor at the London end!'

The evidence was piling up – the heaps of useless florins, the badly forged identity papers, a hundred and one details shamefully neglected. Not to mention the security checks, the inclusion or absence of which did not seem to be noticed. Surely an inquiry would be held after the war?

But the date in our story is 1 July 1942, and the British still had a chance to rouse themselves. At that time, Giskes was jubilant and so was Schreieder, but none in Holland more so than *Reichskommissar* Rauter. A stormy scene was at the origin of it all.

Joseph Schreieder's immediate superior, Harster, had had the bright idea of sending the *England Spiel* file to the *Reichskommissar*. It is strange that he should have made such a grave error, for he knew Rauter's character. He must have realised that the subtleties of espionage and counter-espionage were beyond him. Nor could he have been unaware that Rauter would be furious to learn that the operation had been going on behind his back. But Harster's reason for sending him the file was probably to cover himself with the Himmlerites in case the affair turned into a disaster. The upshot was that on the morning of 4 July Joseph Schreieder was ordered to appear before the *Reichskommissar*, who roundly abused him on three counts:

(1) He, Rauter, expected to be kept informed hourly of everything going on within his department.

(2) An officer who has the signal honour of wearing SS uniform does not get familiar with 'the Jew Canaris's hirelings' (Giskes and his men).

(3) It was unpardonable that Lauwers, Takonis, Baatsen and the others had not yet been tried and shot.

Schreieder listened to this tirade without denying anything. Indeed, his face showed great repentance. But there are lulls in even the worst storms. Rauter at last paused for breath and flicked through the file in front of him.

'*Kriminalrat*, it is obvious that you were acting for the best,' he conceded. 'I know you are a very good police officer. And the capture of the agent Jambroes is not devoid of some useful purpose. In any case, there's no point in stopping now. The 'English Game' must continue. But from now on,' (and he banged the file with his fist) 'I want to be kept informed! You understand? Right, you may go.'

Schreieder clicked his heels and went out, feeling lucky to get off so lightly. He would have been dumbfounded had he known of Rauter's next action.

The *Reichskommissar* called in his private secretary, who could not help noticing the unusually jubilant expression on his face.

'Take a letter,' said the *Reichskommissar*.

It so happened that on 7 July 1942, Himmler received the following communication, which he immediately forwarded to Hitler.

'Reichsführer,

I should like to bring to your notice that the celebrated physics professor Jambroes, who had fled to England and was later parachuted into Holland, has been captured. I have also been successful in capturing all the British agents dropped into Holland.

Jambroes's mission was to recruit about one thousand saboteurs and to organise seventeen districts for sabotage. In addition, he was to be provided with ten instructors and ten radio operators, who are due to be parachuted into Holland in the near future. Their mission is to destroy all our installations in Limburg, Brabant and Gelderland. They will be captured like the others.

In my opinion this clearly demonstrates that the Allies intend to effect a landing in Holland very soon.

Heil Hitler!
Rauter.'

Even if the *England Spiel* had ended there and then, if all the threads that Major Giskes held in his strong hand had suddenly snapped, the operation would still have been the greatest success in German counter-espionage since the beginning of the war. Giskes well deserved the Iron Cross with oak-leaves, swords and diamonds – the decoration awarded to heroes and geniuses, but so sparingly that even Hermann Goering had to intrigue to get it!

But Giskes was not decorated. His role was to remain in the wings. In any case, he had other things on his mind than medals.

By 8 July 1942, he was about the only participant in the *England Spiel* (with Wuhr, who was no fool) still to have doubts about the British, the only one who had not thought of putting a dunce's cap on the Intelligence Service's head.

No, it was too good to be true, the adversary was too compliant. Giskes knew the British. Only someone mad, daft, or blind as a Himmlerite would believe they were bamboozled, that the best organised and the most unscrupulous secret service in the world had fallen into a trap – a clever and well-laid trap, certainly, but not very original. So Giskes kept turning it over in his mind (and he did not know that Lauwers had never once sent his real security check!). There was Jambroes, for instance, and 'Plan Holland' which was found in his pocket, all the instructions written clearly and not even coded. What was behind that? Himmler and his lot believed it meant that a landing in Holland was being planned. But was not that just what the British wanted them to believe?

Giskes tried to reason it out. Most of the British Forces were tied up in North Africa, and the Royal Navy was fully occupied in the Mediterranean theatre with convoy protection. A landing in Europe could therefore be attempted only with very small means. This was bound to lead to disaster for the British. But still, they would surely not have sent a score of men straight into the German trap just to deceive the enemy. Even less would they have sacrificed such a valuable recruit as Jambroes.

Giskes was at a loss – he cogitated and speculated, but no clear ideas emerged. After pondering for some time, he decided to be satisfied with the practical results obtained. The Dutch Resistance had been stifled, the expected support had not arrived and its links with London, the life-line of secret warfare, were broken. In July 1942, the Dutch Resistants were like unseeing insects, roaming about for a time but sooner or later stumbling upon a traitor, a Van der Waals or a Johnny den Droog. Surely that was not what the British wanted!

However, Hermann Giskes had no time to go deeply into the motives and intentions of the men in the opposite camp. London was no longer satisfied just to hold dialogues with its agents, but was demanding action from them. The Germans had found on one agent, Jan Emmer, captured when he parachuted down on

30 June, an order intended for Takonis and instructing him to destroy the powerful radar station at Kootwijk.

Here was a problem for Giskes!

The sabotage of the Kootwijk radar station was intended to be the first action of 'Plan Holland'. German radar had been developed at Kootwijk, which had become a major detection centre and kept check on practically all Allied air and naval activities in the North Sea. The first sabotage operation requested by London was against one of Germany's chief nerve centres! Giskes tried to stall, using Lauwers and Jordaan, but London was insistent and curtly ordered that all available men should be concentrated on this operation, under the command of 'long Thijs'. (He, poor wretch, had not seen the light of day for four months; having committed psychological suicide, he no longer knew about Germans, the British, or even that there was a war on.) For the first time in his career, Giskes found himself forced to improvise. In a way, he was being asked to fire on his own men. And this was only a beginning. An order to execute Major Giskes might be received next.

It was an unprecedented situation for him. In the past, before the war and in Paris during the early months of the German occupation, his 'radio-games' had never lasted long enough to put him in such a predicament. For a moment he thought of breaking off contact, of severing his links with London as one puts down the 'phone. But then he thought of Richard Christmann. . . .

The man might have been a German – he was not very sure himself, and this had always been an advantage. Richard Christmann was one of Major Giskes's very first victims. On the other hand, if Giskes had a friend, it was Christmann (but did Giskes ever have a friend?).

Christmann was born in Alsace-Lorraine of German-speaking parents, and became a French citizen when the province was returned to France after the First World War. He joined the French Foreign Legion, but by 1932 he was active in extremist organisations and going under the name of 'Arnaud'. One day in 1937, during a political demonstration, 'Arnaud' killed a man. The French Deuxième Bureau (counter-espionage) hushed up the matter and so acquired a first-class agent. Christmann was intelligent, bilingual, and had the additional advantages of a frank, open face and a straightforward appearance. He never put on a knowing air or turned up his coat-collar to hide his face. He was the very opposite of Van der Waals, in fact. In 1938 the French sent him to Hamburg to spy on German naval movements. He did some good work for his French masters – until arrested by Giskes.

Christmann, the man without a country, had needed little persuading to work for the *Abwehr*. In any case, it is difficult to see what scruples he could have found. Besides, the Germans paid more than the French. And Giskes had known the right attitude to take with him. These things are important. In short, Arnaud became Christmann again and for some months sent to Paris reports which had been dictated by his German masters.

Since that *Funkspiel*, Richard Christmann had linked his fate with that of Major Giskes. And from the beginning of the *England Spiel* he had been present in the underground radio room at the Citadel, a modest corporal's stripe on the sleeve of his field-green uniform. Giskes told him periodically that he would soon have a job for him, but nothing materialised. Christmann was getting bored, and spent gloomy days going from café to café, picking up a girl or a few bits of information, nothing much.

But suddenly, on 17 July, he found himself back in harness. 'I've got work for you,' Giskes told him. 'You're going to *be* the Dutch Resistance.' Richard Christmann and Hermann Giskes were about to join forces again. These two tricksters, one the counterpart of the other, were going to carry out the orders of the British High Command 'for laughs' – while soldiers were killing one another from Tobruk to Stalingrad, and while men and women were being tortured and shot in prisons and camps all over Europe. Giskes the Prussian and Christmann the Alsatian were going to set fire to Holland – or if not set fire to it, at least to provide a fireworks display. Giskes explained.

The previous day, 16 July, another SOE agent, Aart Hendrik Alblas, had been captured. Giskes and Schreieder had known of his presence for some time but had left him alone because London sent him important messages. If they had arrested him earlier, the charm would have been broken and London would have become suspicious. The moment had not yet come. It came on 16

July, when Alblas received a message telling him to contact Takonis and organise the Kootwijk operation with him.

Schreieder's men had pounced on Alblas as he left his house at Bilthoven fifteen minutes after receiving the message (Alblas never gave anything away, except his name.) Heinrichs took his place at transmission times, then all the radio posts established in Holland by SOE were in Giskes's hands.

However, the Kootwijk radar station had to be blown up, and soon. London was showing signs of impatience. Giskes's attempts to stall, through Lauwers and Jordaan, had been brushed aside. The destruction of Kootwijk was obviously an operation of great urgency on which depended – what? Giskes was deeply intrigued by the insistence of the British.

The Kootwijk installations were undoubtedly of great strategic importance, as they could detect Allied ships approaching the Dutch and German coast or crossing the North Sea. But this hardly justified such feverish impatience, unless Rauter's deduction was correct. Supposing the British were indeed planning a landing on the Dutch coast? That was not Giskes's headache – one of the advantages of secret warfare was to be excluded from top-level planning and overall strategy. But one thing was certain, that the British were unaware of the capture of their agents in Holland. For they would hardly go so far as to instruct men they knew to be in prison to carry out sabotage raids. No, they certainly wouldn't waste their time over such tricks.

A RLS message was sent to London on 1 August: 'Men ready for action.' The reply was, 'Stand by.'

Silence from London on 2 August and on the following day. The British were thinking it over. And Giskes suddenly wondered whether Alblas had been pulled in too late. He could have warned London, and his last message had just been decoded.

In fact, Alblas was arrested in mid-July, and it was now 3 August. It was quite a long time. But Giskes is a pessimist. He studied one after the other all the reasons which could logically have made the English upset the *Funkspiel*. However, it was not unlikely that Alblas's last message had lain a long time on a table before being decoded. At that time, SOE was choked with too many messages but not enough staff, and the agents in occupied territory often had to wait a fortnight or more for replies and instructions relating to their last transmission. Giskes knew this.

RLS signal to London, 4 August: 'Men ready for action stop awaiting precise orders.'

Reply from London: 'Continue standing by.'

This was all very odd, thought Giskes. Only a few days ago London had been so very impatient.

RLS to London, 6 August: 'Men ready to act stop men impatient to act stop awaiting orders end message.'

London replied at once: 'Operation to be carried out August eighth stop Thijs in charge. . . .'

Thijs was instructed to crawl eight hundred yards through a minefield and fix ten pounds of explosive to each radar pylon. London added that they were impatient to receive a report on the raid. Takonis never knew that on the night of 8 August 1942, seven men in a van drove up to within a few hundred yards of Kootwijk radar station, stopped and got out, each man carrying a parcel that looked a little too neat, a little too carefully tied. Their too-new leather jackets shone in the darkness. Each man was armed with a machine-pistol. It was half an hour after midnight when they spread out across the fields. Just before one o'clock, the first shots were heard. The sentries replied with several bursts of machine-gun fire. The skirmish continued for a quarter of an hour. There was considerable firing, but no cries or shouts as usually occurred in attacks of this nature.

When they withdrew, the 'Resistance men' threw a few Mills grenades which were extremely noisy. The play-acting was over, and all the cast, both German soldiers and Dutch traitors, had played their parts very well, with proper moderation. While in a hut not far away, a little group of real Resistance men, whom Schreieder had been at pains to leave at liberty, could bear witness that seven heroes had attacked the Kootwijk garrison but had been beaten off, almost certainly suffering casualties.

'Plan Holland' had got under way.

The following night *they* returned to the attack. Christmann and Kupp had a larger force this time, but it was still blank cartridges that were used and the sentries had again been given orders to fire in the air. Giskes thought two performances of this farce were quite sufficient. On 10 August he sent the following RLS message to London:

'Kootwijk raid unsuccessful stop some of our men ran into a

minefield stop explosions and shots exchanged with sentries stop five of ours missing stop Thijs and two wounded safe stop.'

This would certainly be borne out by any message that the Resistance might have sent. However, London did not bite. The reply made no mention of the Kootwijk raid. The British were suspicious, there could be no doubt. Something had come unstuck – but what? (For five months, it must be remembered, RLS had been sending messages without including his real security check.) Giskes decided to give a final touch to his fabrication. He had Jordaan send the following message on 11 August:

'Two of the five missing from Kootwijk raid have returned stop sentries been increased stop have broken contact stop no indication that enemy on our tracks end message.'

Christmann, who had organised the whole show, could not understand what had gone wrong. Everything had been perfectly arranged – perhaps too perfectly.

Giskes, with his usual clarity, reckoned it was ten to one against London swallowing his story. The machine had seized up, which was only to be expected after five months. As to why it had seized up – he dared not put the everlasting question, had the British finally understood?

Lauwers had informed the British, quite distinctly and four times in quick succession, that he had been captured. All to no purpose.

Other agents—Emmer, Ortt, De Jonge, Brinkman, Radema, Van Steen, Parlevliet, Van Hemert, Jambroes – had still dropped into the arms of *Kriminalrat* Joseph Schreieder.

However, now that he had Jordaan working next to him and with him, Lauwers had taken new hope – an unfounded hope, but without it he would have fallen into the smiling prostration in which Takonis had taken refuge.

Heinrichs had become increasingly strict and interfering since the evening when Lauwers had given him a fright, and it was now impossible to escape his supervision for a moment. But one evening when Lauwers and Jordaan walked unfettered into the underground radio room they found Heinrichs absent and in his place, by their two transmitters, were a couple of sergeants – two pairs of lynx-like eyes, and ears with long lobes that protruded below their headphones. Neither man was young, and at first glance seemed better suited for real warfare, under an open sky, than for the subtle games of espionage.

Jordaan and Lauwers felt they had become prisoners again. Giskes must have decided to set watchdogs over them. (Heinrichs had been denounced by a colleague who had seen him chatting with the two Dutchmen, and he risked being sent to the Eastern front for this negligent conduct. In any case, it would be a long time before Lauwers and Jordaan saw him again.) However, the two new overseers were excellent W/T technicians but knew nothing whatever about the coding system in use. And it was Jordaan, Giskes being absent, who taught them! The two elderly sergeants listened attentively and took notes. They had probably been told that the two Dutchmen were model collaborators. Despite their stern looks, the two Germans were not at all suspicious.

So it was that the following incredible incident took place. The scheduled transmission time was drawing near, and Lauwers started tuning in to the London frequency 'to show them how things were done'. He made contact. London was ready to receive him, in some dilapidated country house northwest of London a signaller was waiting, headphones on and pencil poised.

Lauwers did not waste a second. While the two Germans nodded their understanding of the demonstration he tapped out:

'8, 4, 5, 17, 13, 10, 11, 2, 9, 12, 6, 3, 14, W-O-R-K-E-D-B-Y Y-N-R D R-I-E ...'

'Worked by,' he had sent. The two Germans were listening to the Morse, but did not understand and in any case thought that Lauwers was just practising. Jordaan was scared stiff. Lauwers knew from experience that panic spreads, so avoided looking at him and pressed on:

'N-E-I-N-S-T O-P-E-I-N D-J-E-R-R Y-S-I-N-C E-M ...'

'Jerry since ...' Lauwers had sent out half of a sentence that he had been turning over in his head for weeks. 'Worked by Jerry since ...' Jordaan would never have dared do it, and secretly admired him.

Lauwers was about to send the rest, but one of the watchdogs stopped him. 'That'll do! We understand. Now transmit properly.' Lauwers would have to send his SOS in serial form – continued next day. But even if he were unable to send the rest of the sentence, the British – unless their operators were deaf, blind, or traitors – had received enough of it to put an end to the deadly game.

Luck was with him the following day. He said that something was wrong with the Morse key and politely asked the two Germans for permission to test his set. They consulted together, then the elder nodded to Lauwers. 'All right, but be quick about it!'

Hubertus found the frequency and almost at once made contact with London. This time he sent the complete message:

'Worked by Jerry since March Sixth Jeffers May Third.'

'Stop!' cried the German. 'That's enough.' And, to frighten Lauwers, he glared at him and barked, 'What have you just sent?'

Jordaan was in a cold sweat. Lauwers raised his drawn, tired face. 'I told them I'm fed up with working for two bosses at the same time and I asked for a rise.'

'Lauwers! This is no time for joking! I want an answer! What did you just send?'

Lauwers stood up, took off his headphones and held them out to the German.

'In the first place, I've always been addressed as Lieutenant Lauwers. Secondly, I didn't send any message. You could see for yourself that I tapped out any old thing. But if you don't believe me, you can always transmit in my place. I shan't mind. I warn you, though, I shall complain to Major Giskes.'

He had a nerve, did Lauwers. But, thought the two Germans, for this frail little man to speak to them in such a tone he must assuredly be in the right. The other soldiers in the large room had turned from their work at the sound of the dispute. The guardian angels of Lauwers and Jordaan were making themselves look ridiculous.

'All right, all right,' said the elder. 'Get back to your set. You'll hear more about this later.'

But nothing more was heard about it. 'Plan Holland' had been launched the previous day, and Giskes had more to do than bother with disciplinary matters.

It was 10 August 1942, and inexplicably, despite the excellent party Giskes had put on at Kootwijk, London refused to jump at the bait.

'*Worked by Jerry since March Sixth Jeffers May Third.*'

Having sent this to the British, Lauwers knew they must be

stirring. He was well placed to know, the only person to know that a certain message from RLS had set things humming and that, while the Germans were anxiously speculating, the great secret organisation was being overhauled and given a new structure. He also felt proud at having upset Giskes's game with just a little help from Jordaan. But how would the Germans react when they discovered the breakdown of their operation? (Lauwers still had the major's words in mind – 'I promise that your life will be spared so long as you are working for us.') In a day or a week from now, he and his comrades would become completely useless. And then they would be shot. Just that.

But if the Germans found out that it was he and his friend Jordaan who had warned the British, then the SS might well precede the execution with one of those special sessions in which they took such delight. For the first time since he had begun cooperating with the *Abwehr*, Lauwers felt the physical fears of a normal man.

On 11 August London replied to RLS:

'Greatly regret your failure and losses stop cease all activity pending further orders stop utmost vigilance needed for a time stop inform us of everything you discover message ends.'

Lauwers may have been wrong to consider this message as an order to himself, but to his mind it was clear enough. He took 'utmost vigilance needed' to mean 'we have understood and are being cautious'; and 'inform us of everything you discover' as 'continue your work as though nothing had happened'. And he concluded that they had not let him down after all, and had not let the others down. They were trying to save them.

But there was more to come. The British could not resist ending on a wry note, and on 13 August informed Thijs Takonis, via Lauwers, that 'in view of his heroic action during the Kootwijk raid he would be awarded a decoration at the end of hostilities'. Lauwers thought there might be more to the message than appeared, that it was surely one more move to lull any suspicions that the Germans had.

Schreieder, however, burst out laughing when he heard of it. Giskes the northerner, the prude, merely smiled. But he, too, might have been wondering whether the British were playing him at his own game. Giskes said nothing to anyone, but this reply seemed odd to him; less than a week previously, the British had been eager for the start of 'Plan Holland', but suddenly they began to mark time. Why? (He did not suspect Lauwers; he had stopped suspecting him five months ago.) The dismissive laugh of the *Kriminalrat* seemed to Giskes to be completely irrelevant. He had been crossing swords with British Intelligence for many years and knew what unscrupulous schemers those people were – it would not have been the first time they had decorated a corpse to demonstrate their good faith. Anyway, there was one definite fact – they were not sending any more agents!

What was Giskes's next move to be? At this stage in events, he could see two lines of action: he could break contact with London, hang up all his radio links (he was in possession of eight at this time). The prisoners would be left to Rauter's discretion – their fate was easily imagined.

The advantages were, first, he would not be abandoning the operation because he was defeated. On the contrary, he would have achieved the finest coup in the *Abwehr*'s history. So he had nothing to fear from his superiors and no harm was caused to his self-esteem. And second, he would avoid the risk of being taken in by SOE, who, knowing he was bogged down by this affair, would be free to launch other operations.

The disadvantages were, first, he would never really know if the British had been duped or not. Second, it was obvious (since 'Plan Holland' had come to his knowledge) that they were planning something. But what? Operation North Pole might enable him to find out. Third, at a time when clearsighted people were beginning to notice the winds of change (the Germans were on the defensive in Russia and at their last gasp in North Africa), it was not a good thing to have the execution of a score of Allied agents on one's conscience. (In the summer of 1942, many *Abwehr* officers already had their minds on something like the Nuremberg Trials.)

His second alternative was to continue with his radio game, prolonging the dialogue with the enemy in an atmosphere of complete candour. He would at least be misleading the British. Besides, they surely did not suspect that *all* their radio posts were in German hands. He could continue to play back other transmitters than those of Lauwers and Jordaan. There were hardly any disadvantages: he would not be running any great risk by continuing the game. The only headache would be if the British wanted more raids carried out. If they gave orders for German soldiers to be attacked in the streets, which was not not unlikely, it would be difficult to satisy them.

Giskes's cogitations came to an end here. He decided to continue with his *England Spiel*.

So Richard Christmann appeared on the scene again. Imagine workpeople in Rotterdam coming out of offices and factories for the lunch break, one August day in 1942. Only a few go home, some sit in the sun, eating a sandwich; others stroll along the banks of the grey river Lek and see a tug flying the Swastika drawing a barge carrying three or four aircraft. Although they were covered over with a large tarpaulin, the shape of the planes was evident; and as the barge drew nearer, the tail of a Messerschmidt-109 was seen protruding from under the tarpaulin. There was something absurd in this spectacle of some of the fastest planes in the world being conveyed by the slowest means of transport.

Suddenly, as the tug was about to pass under a bridge, a sharp explosion rent the air; the tarpaulin flew off and the barge listed to starboard with thick smoke pouring from it. The onlookers, after a moment of startled surprise, began to laugh and clap. Someone shouted, 'Bravo, the Resistance!'

'That'll teach the Boches!' came another cry.

Some police hurried towards the small crowd, truncheons drawn, and soon broke up the demonstration.

A hundred yards away, Major Giskes was putting his binoculars back in their case. He turned to the man with him. 'Nice work, my dear Christmann, we've just devised the Dutch Resistance!'

Richard Christmann had boarded the barge an hour earlier, accompanied by alleged civil engineers. They had placed the explosive charges after satisfying themselves that there would be no one aboard the barge during its tow up the river with the crashed aircraft (for they were, of course, good only for scrap).

Giskes and Christmann had told no one in advance, not even German naval headquarters. (Imagine trying to explain the subtleties of counter-espionage to a typical *Kriegsmarine* officer!) And they had done the right thing. The following day, all the

Dutch newspapers controlled by the Germans carried the story of 'the cowardly attack, which fortunately caused no casualties, perpetrated by terrorists in the pay of the British'. It was reported that 'deep concern was felt among the population'.

More important still, a week later a copy of the clandestine paper *Het Parool* fell into the hands of the Gestapo and was found to contain an item on 'the heroic action of the soldiers without uniform'. The Resistance – and consequently British Intelligence – had no doubts that the sabotage was the work of SOE agents.

The Rotterdam job, however, had not been carried out at the request of London. Giskes had taken the initiative into his own hands. As the British had ceased calling for direct action, he would do it for them. They seemed to have lost trust in him, so he would prove that the Dutch were quite capable, with or without orders from Baker Street, of carrying out subversive activities. There would be more to come. Christmann, playing it cool in this gigantic farce, thought he had been given a wonderful chance – while three-quarters of the German Army were being badly mauled trying to hold the Russians in the mud and the British in the desert sands, he was able to have his own little war without any risk of being killed or even wounded. And the British had supplied the wherewithal by dropping their containers filled with arms and explosives.

Giskes's directive to Christmann had been as follows: 'It's most important that the British should be made aware of the existence of an organised secret force in Holland. When they ask me for a report on the activities of this or that agent, I want to be able to reply that he blew up a bridge a day or two ago. And I want that bridge actually to have been blown. Get it?'

On the night of 21 August 1942, the inhabitants of Breda were startled from sleep by a series of loud explosions. It was not bombs falling; the noises were of quite a different sort. Hundreds of windows were blown out, big reddish-yellow flames were seen on the skyline, and the fires seemed to be spreading. More explosions were heard. It was an hour before all the flames and noise died down.

Christmann had used explosives, barrels of gunpowder and some fireworks, placed round a coal heap which had been drenched with petrol, to make everyone in the district believe that an ammunition train had been blown up!

On 23 August a reasonable amount of dynamite was used to blow up a disused railway track just outside Arnhem. The newspapers, informed by Giskes, gave credence to rumours that railway communications between Arnhem and the nearby German frontier area would be badly disrupted for a week.

On 25 August, in one of the main streets of Utrecht, some young men opened fire on German soldiers on leave. The soldiers returned the fire, while people scattered and dived into doorways. Miraculously, no one was killed or even wounded. Christmann and his assistants alone knew that blanks had been fired. Every two or three days, Giskes and Christmann provided evidence of the existence of an army in the shadows.

But while thousands of men were being killed on every war front, while partisans were attacking the enemy in Yugoslavia and the Maquis in France, Belgium, Norway was harassing the occupying forces, it seemed that Resistance activities in Holland were not entirely confined to the tricks of a turncoat working for the *Abwehr*.

Actually, all over the urbanised Netherlands, where fields and polders are like green patches sewn on red trousers (what could the word 'maquis' mean in Holland?), there existed a very real Resistance movement. But for many months its members had not received a single container of arms and ammunition. Schreieder and his men seized them all as soon as they were dropped.

The Resistance members awaited instructions, but in vain. Nevertheless, they took action – blindly, without any plan, without any guiding tactics. They emerged at dusk, revolvers in hand, and fired on German patrols or groups of collaborators. They were very often Jews, driven by despair rather than inspired by a cause. Whenever these heroes were captured, the Gestapo did not mince matters. They were tortured and shot, and they died thinking they were forgotten men (were they so very far wrong?).

Schreieder and his men sometimes found printed instructions and advice in the containers which dropped at their feet:

'Place this tube of grease in the axle of a train; when the wheel begins to turn, a fire will be started.'

'This delayed-action bomb will start a fire half-an-hour after your departure.'

'Fix this magnetic limpet mine to the hull of a warship, about one yard from her bows. The delaying action can be adjusted, from ten minutes to four hours.'

'If this hand-grenade is concealed in an aircraft, it will explode under the effect of atmospheric compression at a height of 1,500 feet.'

'Break into a German Army laundry (sic) and sprinkle this finely-powdered glass over the soldiers' shirts. Irritating effect guaranteed; unbearable itching, outbreak of rashes, pimples, etc.'

The real Dutch Resistance fighters would never set eyes on these hand-grenades and limpet mines. They would die before knowing anything about these gadgets, and in great numbers, youngsters for the most part, ignorant of the real state of affairs.

Lauwers, Takonis, Jordaan, Pijl, Akki, Van Steen, Baatsen, Jambroes and the rest – it was about time you realised! In this great world war, you just did not count!

You had been told enough times during your training – you were expendable, tools that could be replaced. You had been made into heroes. What more did you want? To be saved? You were mad.

'Had the British understood or not?' You asked yourself that question a thousand times, Lauwers, but it was quite pointless.

A plan had been decided upon, and officially it was being carried out. That was fine. You shouted that you had been captured, Lauwers, you and your comrades? So what? You didn't count, Lauwers. You had no right to argue with the evidence. And it was evident that all was going according to plan. Night and day, sabotage was being carried out, even before the orders were received. Barges and bridges were blown up, factories and railroads destroyed. You would have been wrong to complain, Lauwers.

And in fact he was not complaining.

Major Giskes, by using false Resistants to blow up installations which did not exist, had regained the confidence of the British. Men and containers were again being dropped into Holland on moonless nights. It was a terrific bluff. Lauwers, sitting at his little transmitter, was again forced to the conclusion that his distress signal had served no purpose. Perhaps the men over there had hesitated for a moment and wondered a little, before being quickly caught up in their mad routine. They were again sending orders that were connected with 'Plan Holland', but this time (as Giskes had feared from the start) the orders were precise and to the point, alarmingly so:

'The following collaborators must be assassinated without delay:

'Van Tonningen, president of the Netherlands Bank and an ardent Nazi.

'Anton Mussert, leader of the Dutch Nazi Party (NSB), and his deputy, Van Geelkerken.

'Ernst Voorhoeve, propaganda chief of the NSB.

'Huygens, chief organiser of the NSB.

'Woudenberg, chief of the Labour Front.

'De Jager, district leader of the NSB.

'Feldmeyer, commander of the Dutch SS.

'Zondervan, commander of the NSB Stormtroops.'

Major Giskes would not have felt the slightest remorse in carrying out the orders to shoot this bunch of collaborators, whom he despised, if it helped to ensure the success of Operation North Pole. And it was simple enough – he had only to tell Ridderhoff to pass on the orders to a real Resistance group. But Giskes had to consider the repercussions, the evils that would come upon him if the Gestapo tracked down the originator of the attacks. The temptation was strong, but it obviously had to be resisted. Although he disliked half-measures, Giskes came to the conclusion that the only thing to do was to temporise. He replied to the British with a message which ought to have made them think again.

'Impossible to attack the men named stop they never travel without strong bodyguard stop impossible shoot Mussert except with telescopic rifle stop do not possess telescopic rifle.'

London promised to send one, but never did.

However, the deaths of Mussert and a few other Dutch collaborators were of no concern just then. For the moment, the chief actor in Operation North Pole was not Giskes nor Schreieder, but Rauter. The *Reichskommissar* had followed up his report to Himmler and had succeeded in convincing him. The head of all the black-uniformed men had become alarmed about the possibility of an Allied landing on the Dutch coast. He had told Hitler, who had informed the High Command. When Rauter asked for reinforcements, Keitel withdrew three mixed divisions from France, Belgium and Norway and sent them to Holland.

On 17 August 1942, three squadrons of bombers from Normandy and the Paris area arrived at Eindhoven in Brabant. On the same day, the coastal batteries were reinforced by two anti-aircraft regiments. The German High Command was turning its eyes from the Russian front only to glance in one direction – at the Dutch coast.

A force of Lancasters bombed The Hague and Rotterdam on the night of 18 August. At daybreak, German machine-gunners, dug in among the sand-dunes, had their fingers on the trigger. *The invasion was coming!* The fever had even reached the prisons, and the inmates were telling one another at exercise-time and over the pipes – the invasion was coming! Another week, and the German High Command would be withdrawing all non-combatant troops from the interior and sending them to man the Dutch coastal defences!

On 19 August 1942, there was indeed an invasion. Not along the Dutch coast, but at Dieppe.

The numbers of Canadian dead left on the pebbly beaches showed that the Jambroes mission and 'Plan Holland' had failed to turn the attention of the German High Command from the Straits of Dover.

10

The Check

The last days of August passed uneventfully. London and Giskes seemed to have nothing more to say to each other; they were merely exchanging routine messages. It was like a love affair petering out, both sides wanting to break it off but unable to find the right words.

The affair had lasted more than five months, and it was not at all clear who emerged as the victor in this secret tussle. But one thing was certain – Major Giskes could show positive results. He held fourteen agents from Britain in his prison, eight of them radio operators and six saboteurs. Among them was an important leader, Jambroes, and the mere fact of his being in Haaren prison still puzzled Giskes. He still had doubts about the intentions of the British. They would never have sent a man like Jambroes, knowing he would fall into the German trap, in the faint hope that the German High Command would thereby conclude that the Allies were planning to land in Holland. Giskes was quite sure of that. No, the British had played into his hand from the very beginning.

But then, what was behind their sudden reserve? Giskes found what was perhaps a valid explanation – the British were getting their breath back before embarking on other operations. Besides, they could not have unlimited reserves of agents and sabotage material. They had not sent so many men and containers to any other occupied country. Probably they were concentrating their efforts elsewhere for the moment – on Belgium or Yugoslavia. But Giskes felt sure that they would soon turn their attention to him again. He could not believe that the break had come.

While waiting for fresh signs of their trust in him, Giskes had given orders to Christmann, Wuhr and their team to intensify their activities. Not a week passed without some junk-heap, classified as an 'ammunition depot', being blown up, or some village footbridge, promoted for the occasion to a bridge of military importance, going sky-high. When Christmann's tricks were seen in conjunction with actual attacks carried out by real Resistants, the effect was that of a Holland being set ablaze. Giskes conscientiously sent reports of all these activities via Lauwers and other links. London replied with cool congratulations, but that was all. The two could hardly be said to have fallen out, but someone was sulking.

Giskes did not take offence. He tried harder, wanting at all costs to regain the confidence of the British. And on 1 September his efforts were rewarded, as witness the following message:

'Congratulations on your successes stop but take special care not to damage the dykes stop sending more agents shortly message ends.'

The game was on again. But, after Dieppe, it was going to be stiffer than ever.

On 7 September London announced that 'a very important agent would shortly be parachuted'. Giskes thought it would be the Jambroes affair all over again. What was the operation in hand now? As he paced up and down the large underground room he could not help wondering whether a trap was being laid for him personally. But that could not be – the British did not know he existed. In theory at least.

Schreieder, whom he met twice a week at the Red Lion Hotel in Amsterdam, was becoming uneasy too. Each time they met, he poured forth his fears. Rauter was demanding tangible results – it couldn't go on like this for much longer. There was talk in the SS mess of *Abwehr* plots against the Himmlerites ('and do you know, my dear comrade, that your 'friend' Admiral Canaris is in semi-disgrace?'). Seyss-Inquart himself was expressing surprise that so many Blackshirts were occupied in spy-hunting instead of putting down terrorism.

Actually, the plump little man was delighted at making Giskes realise that it was he, Schreieder, who was keeping the North Pole business afloat. He did not hide from Giskes – who had always known it, anyway – that at the first sign of trouble, or a purge, he would not raise a finger to help him and would disown him without compunction. At least the *Kriminalrat* was frank.

On 19 September London informed RLS that the agent 'Arie'

would be dropped on the night of the 20th in a field just outside Apeldoorn.

It would be the fifteenth time that an agent had been 'received', and Giskes ought to have overcome his nervousness, but he could not help wondering whether he was walking into a trap. Instead of an agent, a bundle of well-directed bombs might drop on the reception committee. That kind of thing had been known to happen. Only recently, in France, a small group of Gestapo men who went to a dropping zone in the place of captured Resistants had been blown to bits in that way. Schreieder was not very happy either, as he waited on the edge of the field with his police and V-men. Cold, gusty winds had chased away the summer, rain was pouring down, and Schreieder and his men were already wet through. They were bad-tempered, convinced that they had been brought out for nothing. The plane would never find the field through the low clouds, and even if it did, the pilot would hardly dare drop the agent in such a gale.

But by eleven o'clock the wind had died down, and the black clouds parted to disclose a pale mauve sky faintly lit by the moon. It was a kind of miracle, but one that would prove fatal for the unfortunate man about to drop from the sky. Schreieder and his men could hardly believe their eyes. The next few minutes were like a recurring dream – the same sounds, the same scenes, and in particular the same relief when the plane appeared, flying very low and well on time. The agent and the containers came floating down in the normal manner.

Schreieder and his men did not waste time in talk. Contrary to their usual practice, they pounced on the agent at once. He struggled for a moment, but no cry came from him, no curse. He accepted the situation almost at once. He was thrust, handcuffed, into a car, and still uttered no protest. He seemed to be conserving his strength for a more important struggle.

They were back at the Binnenhoff by daybreak, in Schreieder's office, putting their coats round the stove to dry. The man had still not uttered a word. Nothing had been found on him but a badly-forged identity-card, a large amount in florins and the usual box of matches with pills in the false bottom. He was dressed more or less like this predecessors, but Schreieder sensed that he was of a different stamp altogether. They began to interrogate him. Seeing his firm mouth and resolute face, and realising that the man knew his own strength, Schreieder was expecting to meet with a determined refusal to talk and thinking that recourse to torture might be necessary. Schreieder did not like to be present at such scenes.

However, the man talked.

He said his name was Jongelie. 'Arie' was his code-name. He had been despatched by SOE. He answered calmly, without any swagger or bluster. It was as though he was quite prepared for what was happening to him. He showed no surprise.

'Exactly what is your mission?' asked Schreieder.

'I haven't one. My mission is vague.'

'All the same. . . . ?'

'I was to make contact with Resistance groups and try to establish a new radio link.'

'Is that all?'

'That's all.'

'Who were you to meet?'

Jongelie gave names. Schreieder knew who they were – they were men he had already arrested. It seemed too good to be true. Jongelie was an ideal agent – not only did he talk, but all unknowingly it seemed he entered into the 'English Game', and quite naturally, without a protest or a murmur. Very odd.

Schreieder was very tired, after being up all night, and his mental faculties were considerably diminished. He realised this, and decided to call Giskes to his aid.

The major arrived at the Binnenhoff at about ten o'clock. He was in a foul temper, for he hated to be seen in uniform in the Gestapo offices. But he could hardly refuse the *Kriminalrat*'s request and, besides, they had common interests. He had to find out as soon as possible what was being hidden by the unnaturally self-possessed, polite and compliant Roleof Christian Jongelie. Schreieder could manage tough men very well, but he was out of his element when he had to deal with a courteous prisoner. A too evident frankness put him off his balance. Giskes, on the other hand, was adept at dislodging the base on which a whole falsehood rested. Schreieder had given Giskes a brief description of the man over the telephone, and Giskes had thought that the Gestapo had once again arrested a man who was too much for them.

He walked straight into Schreieder's office and asked to be left alone with the prisoner. Then he sat down opposite Jongelie and looked him stonily in the eye. Jongelie had spent many years in the Dutch East Indies and had there learned a number of ways of controlling his emotions. It needed more than Major Giskes's steely gaze to disconcert him.

'Mr Arie,' Giskes began.

'You may call me Jongelie, you know. Arie is my code name, and if I have understood correctly I shan't need it any more. . . .'

He said it quite pleasantly and with no trace of sarcasm. Giskes was thrown out of his stride.

'Whoever you are,' he said in a harsher tone, 'I suppose you ought to inform your superiors that you have arrived safe and sound.'

'Quite so, Major. That's right, isn't it? You are a major?'

'Yes. I suppose, in fact I'm sure, that you have a code signal to indicate that all is well and that you are free. All your comrades had one.' (Giskes purposely said 'had', to imply that they were dead, which might have some effect on 'Arie'.) But Jongelie showed not the slightest emotion. 'Yes, indeed,' he calmly admitted. 'I was given a code signal, as you say.'

'Tell me what it is,' said Giskes.

He was expecting Jongelie to give a laugh and say – as Van der Reyden had – 'What do you take me for?'

But Jongelie looked up at the ceiling as though making a great effort to remember. 'I'll think of it in a moment. Don't rush me. I'm going to tell you. Ah yes, I remember – "The express left on time." It has to be repeated.'

The man was either very clever, or else it was an almost unique instance of spontaneous 'turning'.

Giskes dismissed the second idea, for Jongelie had forgotten to conceal something of great importance – his high intelligence. It shone from his face. Moreover, he did not look a coward, a weakling. His head and bull-neck, his powerful arms and shoulders were those of a fighter. And yet the SS who had captured him said that he had not put up any struggle. It didn't hang together.

The truth was as clear as day: the British must have sent 'Arie' to check up on the radio posts which London thought might be 'burnt'.

Giskes returned to the attack. 'May I know why you have told me your code signal without the slightest hesitation?'

Jongelie drew a deep breath and again seemed to be racking his brain for the reply.

'It's quite simple,' he said. 'I know that no one can hold out against your methods. If you had tortured me, I should have talked, like everyone else. So why suffer so much pain? And in any case . . .' He paused.

'In any case what?' snapped Giskes.

'In any case – well, we've won the war. It may take another six months or perhaps ten years. But anyway, you're beaten. So it's as one of the victorious side – the future victorious side – that I'm talking to you. To a man of your intelligence, it must be obvious. So let's say that I want to stay alive to see our victory.'

Giskes did not at all like the calm and reasonable manner in which 'Arie' made his statement. He shouted: 'And what makes you think that I shall let you stay alive?'

'Because, Major, unless I'm greatly mistaken, you're going to need me.'

Two hours later Giskes was back in his own office at the Citadel, a setting which was much more to his liking, even though he was not alone. Fifty pairs of eyes watched the newcomer pass by. Jongelie's demeanour had not changed. Behind his immobile features there seemed to be some inner serenity. In a matter of hours his beard had begun to show here and there.

Giskes called for coffee. There was no atmosphere of interrogation here, and the major placed great hopes in the friendly surroundings of his private den. But Jongelie was no Lauwers, even less a Jordaan. Nor Akki, nor Pijl either. The British had not sent an idealist this time. Reasoning and moralising would have no effect on him. Other methods were needed to draw him into the mad round of the North Pole game. In fact, it was not a matter of persuading him. He had entered it of his own accord, and therein lay his strength.

Giskes's problem was simple – had Jongelie given him the correct message expected in London to announce his safe arrival? He was sure he had not. If Christmann were captured in Manchester or Portsmouth, he would act in the same way.

'At what time should you send the message to London?' asked Giskes.

'At eleven this morning. But, as you probably know, a short delay is permissible.'

These remarks, such as 'as you probably know', 'you are doubtlessly aware', and 'unless I'm greatly mistaken', with which Jongelie sprinkled his conversation, were getting on the major's nerves. The man seemed to be making himself at home in the *Abwehr* headquarters.

Giskes was playing against time (if he waited too long to send the message, even until the afternoon, the British would again become suspicious). He was also playing against himself, resisting the temptation to take Jongelie by the coat-collar and bang his head against the wall until he told the truth. However, Giskes still held a strong card, and he was about to play it.

Jongelie's transmitter, which had been found in one of the containers, was standing on a side-table. It was the same toylike apparatus in a black case as had been given to Lauwers and Jordaan. A corporal had plugged it in and was jiggling the Morse key.

Giskes had less than an hour to spare. He ordered Jongelie's handcuffs to be taken off and asked him to sit down, then offered him a cigarette which was accepted.

'You know that I'm taking a tremendous risk in sending the code signal you've given me?' said Giskes.

'Oh? How is that, Major?'

'Because it's ten to one that those words mean you've been captured!'

Not a muscle moved on Jongelie's face. He replied in a polite drawing-room manner, with the slightest trace of self-satisfaction.

'Oh, you're quite mistaken, Major. Only if my chiefs heard nothing from me would they believe I'd fallen into German hands. Just think. Where would they suppose I was transmitting from? My prison cell? I assure you that my chiefs know nothing of your methods. They haven't the slightest suspicion that some of their agents are working for you.'

That was Jongelie's first mistake. Giskes pounced upon it.

'And what makes *you* think we're using captured agents?'

'But it's obvious.' Jongelie made a wide gesture to include the whole of the *Abwehr* headquarters. 'One had only to come in here to realise. Unless I'm greatly mistaken, you've captured one or more SOE agents. He or they gave you their code, you've been exchanging messages with London in their place, and that's how you were able to capture me.'

Jongelie certainly had a nerve! And his reasoning was perfect. It denoted a high intelligence, which he obviously had. Or else it was the British who had told him the whole story.

'All right,' said Giskes. 'Then perhaps you'll tell me why you are prepared to join the game.'

'I've told you – I want to live. I want to see the end of the war. And – correct me if I'm wrong – I shall remain alive so long as I'm useful to you.'

To all appearances, Major Giskes was caught in his own trap. Jongelie had an answer to everything, and Giskes had failed to take advantage of his mistake when he let slip that he knew a lot, a lot too much. Giskes had allowed himself to fall in with Jongelie's ways. Nothing is more difficult than to corner a man who offers no resistance. However, the longer they talked the clearer did Jongelie's mission become. Giskes now had no doubt whatever that he had been sent to check on some of the radio links in Holland.

The hour was approaching. It was five minutes to eleven when Giskes handed a sheet of paper to the corporal sitting in front of the agent's transmitter.

'Put this into code,' he said, 'and send it at eleven o'clock exactly.'

The corporal read : 'The express left on time.'

Giskes was leaning over the soldier and had his back to Jongelie. He did not hear a sound from behind, nor did he feel that anyone was staring at him (Jongelie was sitting about three yards behind him). The prisoner was not tied, but there were plenty of soldiers in the room to overpower him if he tried to commit suicide or kill someone. But Giskes never gave a thought to that kind of danger.

So it was on instinct and more particularly because he was sure of what he would see, that Giskes suddenly turned round.

He just caught sight of the smile on Jongelie's face.
So the message he had given meant treachery.

Giskes snatched the paper from the corporal, who was already trying to make contact.

'Don't send that! Stop!'

He thought for a moment, then dictated to the corporal loudly and distinctly so that everyone could hear.

'Send this instead: "Accident occurred Operation Parsley" ('Arie's' mission) "stop Arie landed heavily and is unconscious stop he is safe and in good hands stop doctor diagnosed severe concussion stop further report will follow stop." That's the end of it.'

Then he turned to Jongelie. 'When I told you, Mr Jongelie, that we were going to bring about your death. . . .'

The agent was not the same man that Schreieder had captured a few hours previously. He, too, was about to succumb to despair. The superhuman self-control he had learned in far-away Dutch colonies was visibly abandoning him. His mission had ended in failure. He was of no use now. So why keep the mask on?

Jongelie was weeping.

Three days later, Giskes sent another message:

'Arie regained consciousness yesterday but only briefly stop doctor has hopes of slight improvement message ends.'

'Arie' was dying. In Russia, Von Paulus was making a pincer movement on Stalingrad. The Eighth Army was advancing across Libya, and the Americans had decided to land in Morocco. Viewed against such events, what did the death of 'Arie' matter?

On 20 September 1942, Giskes reported to London:

'Arie died suddenly yesterday without regaining consciousness stop we will bury him on the moors stop hope to give him worthy memorial after victory is won message ends.'

Jongelie, in prison, was told of 'Arie's' fate by Giskes himself. Jongelie asked for the names of the men who had betrayed him, but Giskes refused to give them.

Christmann and his gang actually went one night and dug a grave on the moors near Apeldoorn, and lowered into it a ply-wood coffin filled with earth. Some of the Resistance could have been watching the ceremony from a distance, so care was taken with the solemn demeanour appropriate to secret burials of this kind. Christmann and his recruits stood with heads bowed before filling in the hole.

What macabre irony! A sham funeral held in a country where the Germans were daily murdering scores of innocent people! This secret warfare had reached a point where it was nothing but an uncouth caricature of the dramas of the real war. It had turned into a melodrama which was bound to have a bloody ending. It could not be otherwise.

The death of 'Arie' removed the last doubts of the British, if indeed they ever had any.

In October 1942, they parachuted nine agents into Holland! Never before had they despatched so many in a single month.

The agents' names were: Peter Kamphorst, Meindert Koolstra, Michel Pals, Jan Hoofstede, Christiaan Pouwels, Reinder Steeksma, Max Humphrey Macrae, Jacob Bakker and Cornelius Dane.

Operation North Pole was working better than ever.

11

Contagion

Immediately after the death of 'Arie' London asked for news of Jambroes, the chief organiser of 'Plan Holland'. To the British, he appeared to be extremely efficient. Christmann, acting in his name, had made a hero of him. SOE wanted him to return to England, for a man of his stamp and worth could not be left indefinitely exposed to dangers!

On 28 October, Giskes received the following message:

'Find replacement Jambroes stop prepare landing ground for air pick up message ends.'

To which Giskes replied: 'Seeking suitable landing ground stop difficult replace Jambroes for the moment.'

Giskes was temporising, but not in order to find a way out of a difficulty this time. He had in mind a vast plan which would extend far beyond Holland. By using Jambroes and his mission, Giskes intended to spread the North Pole contagion throughout Occupied Europe, to infiltrate his agents into Belgian and French Resistance groups and so into Britain.

Giskes was a practical man. Officially, the means at his disposal were very limited. And it would seem that he, a mere major, had already exceeded his powers in fabricating an active Dutch Resistance. How could he hope to do more? What was the meaning of the smile on the major's face in those early days of November 1942?

Giskes's evasive replies were exhausting London's patience. Their messages became insistent, messages beginning with 'How is it that . . . ?' or 'We do not understand why . . .' Their request was simple enough, a landing ground for a Lysander to pick up Jambroes. The radio exchanges went on for some weeks, winter was approaching, but the major was even more sure of himself and continued to maintain that an air 'pick up' was impossible in

Holland 'in the prevailing conditions'. At the end of the year, the British – who were still despatching agents, all of whom fell unfailingly into Schreieder's net – asked Giskes to arrange a 'pick up' by sea. He replied that the construction of the Atlantic Wall and the reinforcement of air and naval defences in Holland put such an operation out of the question.

His object in all this was quite simple. He was hoping that SOE would despatch a special team to Holland to organise Jambroes's journey *by land*. As these agents were almost certain to be captured, Giskes would then control the escape route and could use it to send men of his own choice to England. One can imagine the kind of people an *Abwehr* chief would have liked to send to England in 1942!

On 18 January 1943, Schreieder's men arrested two Dutch agents who had been instructed by London to organise escape routes. The two were tortured, and gave a mass of names and 'safe houses' established along the routes, in Belgium, Switzerland and France as well as in Holland. Giskes at once informed London that Jambroes would return to England 'through France and Spain, as troop concentrations and police controls ruled out any other route'. After some hesitation, London accepted the inevitable. Giskes had got what he wanted!

One February morning, the major sent for Christmann. The latter found his chief all excited and with a glint of mischief in those steely blue eyes. As usual when at the start of an important operation, Giskes gave his instructions in short, sharp sentences, very much to the point, frequently stroking his moustache with his forefinger as if to hold back a laugh. First, Christmann would drop his own name and revert to that of Arnaud, which had been his mother's maiden name. His first move would be to infiltrate into an escape line by passing himself off as a Frenchman from a frontier region on whom the war had brought many misfortunes (he would in fact become his natural self again). Everything then depended on how things turned out. If all went well, another triumph would be gained over British Intelligence.

Christmann-Arnaud had little difficulty in finding where some baled-out Allied airmen were in hiding in Amsterdam. Giskes had decided to inaugurate the escape line by repatriating men who knew nothing whatever about underground warfare and so would praise Arnaud's organisation to the skies.

One evening in February, Arnaud and an accomplice burst into an attic where a RAF bomber pilot and his gunner were hiding, shivering with cold and half-starved. Arnaud had known about them for some time. They had been shot down six weeks previously, been taken to this empty house by some Resistance men and left to look after themselves. They crept out at night to steal food, and were in an indescribably filthy state. Their immediate reaction was that the Gestapo had come for them, and one made to draw his revolver. But Arnaud quickly put out a hand as though to bless him and said in English: 'We are friends. Here are some clean clothes. Get dressed quickly. Don't ask any questions. We're taking you to a safer place.'

When they were ready, Arnaud stuffed their pockets with identity cards, passes, ration cards and money – enough to travel in safety all round Europe. They were full of gratitude, once they had recovered from their fright and astonishment. Before leaving, Arnaud made them learn by heart a long list of contacts in Belgium and France, half of whom were genuine Resistants and the rest men in the pay of the Germans. Early the following morning, Arnaud put the two airmen on the train to Liège. Three weeks later, they reached London. (They are still unaware that their escape was engineered by a major in the *Abwehr*.)

During the next few weeks, other baled-out airmen followed the same route (Liège-Paris-Port Bou-Barcelona-Madrid-Gibraltar-London), and all reported that the Arnaud escape line worked perfectly smoothly. London was quick in sending congratulations via RLS, 'Turnip', 'Swede' and other links firmly held by Giskes.

However, London was still asking for Jambroes to return to England. The man was becoming an encumbrance, so Giskes decided to kill him off as he had 'Arie'. He sent a brief message to London: 'Jambroes disappeared on mission stop almost certainly dead message ends.'

London swallowed this; and Christmann was able to use his fake escape line to send Allied airmen and German agents and Resistants both real and false to England. Giskes was careful to vary the dose, mixing the quality of the 'escapees' as well as changing the numbers in each party. His *England Spiel* was developing. Christmann even dug out an exemplary Resistance member, a man named Knoppers whom he had met in an Amsterdam café the previous summer. Christmann had been 'working' on him since then, and had managed to convince him that he, Christmann, was a kind of envoy extraordinary of Queen Wilhelmina. One day, Christmann told Knoppers that he had been chosen by Her Majesty to go to London and give a detailed report on the situation in Holland. It must be remembered that the Dutch Resistance was completely in the dark at this period; forgotten and ignored, hoping for help from the skies that never came, its members were easily duped. Knoppers blushed with pride and suspected nothing. Aided by Christmann, he was soon on his way to London. When he reached Britain he was clamped in detention before he had time to give a vivid description of her oppresed country to the Queen of Holland. A fortnight passed before he was interrogated. Knoppers said, in all good faith, that he had come on a special mission at the request of the Queen of Holland. The British Intelligence officers did not deem it necessary to inform Queen Wilhelmina, and Knoppers was sent to join a Free Dutch infantry regiment to help him forget all he had seen and done during the past three years. And he never had an opportunity to deliver the fine speech he had prepared for Queen Wilhelmina.

It was all very sad. But for every honest and trusting Knoppers, how many of the Christmann kind were infiltrated into Britain by the *Abwehr*? This is a secret that Giskes will carry with him to the grave.

The most tragic results of the operation, however, were to occur in Paris. At the end of February 1943, Giskes decided it was time to rid himself of Jambroes's 'successor', a fictitious person of his own invention whose imaginary exploits he had been regularly reporting to London. Like Jambroes, Anton – the name Giskes had given him – had become an encumbrance. London was urgently asking him to go to England for consultations. Giskes prepared to kill him off too, and informed London, over the 'Golf' radio post, that the 'chief' was on his way.

Giskes gave his version of the events in the book he wrote after the war :

'The part of Anton was played by my excellent assistant, Bo . . .'[1] Arnaud accompanied this 'chief' to Paris, where they were accepted by SOE agents on giving the password previously arranged with

---

[1] Sergeant Karl Boden, of the *Abwehr* office at Driebergen, who spoke fluent Dutch. (cf. *Inside SOE*, by E. H. Cookridge).

London. Shortly before the 'chief' was due to leave for England, he was arrested by German Field Police during a 'routine' check at a café on the Boulevard des Italiens. Arnaud and a British radio operator named 'Marcel', who were present at the time, were allowed to go free. 'Marcel' reported the arrest to London, deploring the fate of the 'heroic Dutchman'.[2]

Boden was of course released the same evening by the Paris *Abwehr*. Giskes omitted to add in his book that this vaudeville act soon brought tragedy to the SOE network in France. The Gestapo were put on the track of many agents, and a few months later carried out wholesale arrests. Their extent can be gauged from the fact that they became known as 'the disaster to the French Section'.

This was, alas, only a beginning. The blood of valiant men in Holland was soon to flow too.

---

[2] *Londres Appelle Pole Nord*, by H. J. Giskes. Plon, Paris, 1958.

12

The Deadly Thrust

Giskes was feeling triumphant, but Schreieder was none too happy. He felt that he was neglecting his proper work. Counter-espionage was exciting, and the machinations of Major Giskes thrilled him, but while he was chasing after spies he was not doing his job as a policeman. He had been sent to Holland to hunt down Resistants (as a few years previously he had hunted down Jews and Communists in the Sudeten – and, God knows, he had achieved good results!). He was just a copper – as his chief, Harster, regularly told him – and he ought to be doing a copper's job.

For months, the voluble little Bavarian had been hoping that the 'English Game' would give him the means of strangling the Dutch Resistance movement once and for all. This had been at the back of his mind when he agreed to collaborate with the *Abwehr* in March 1942.

He had set up his own radio detection service without inform-ing Giskes or anyone else. All the flirting with the British, play-ing back transmitters and turning agents, those hundred-and-one manoeuvres in order to capture lone agents – it was not really worth it (so Schreieder thought). He dreamed of roping in the whole of the Resistance at one fell swoop, of seeing all the leaders, their lieutenants and their men struggling in one great net.

Schreieder knew that the Dutch Resistance movement was double-headed. One of the leaders, Vorrink, was the organiser, the brains of the movement. The other, who called himself D'Aquin, was the man of action. Schreieder had sworn to get both of them.

D'Aquin, whose real name was Vermeulen, was no amateur. He had been a police inspector before the war, and had learned a lot about police methods from the Germans themselves, when on a course in Hamburg. He had become the most respected of the leaders of *Orde Dienst*, a right-wing political organisation which had gone underground in 1941. Many regular army officers had joined *Orde Dienst*, which was undoubtedly the best organised and best led of all the Dutch Resistance groups. But order and discipline were of little use when the leaders had no contact with the outside world and lacked arms and ammunition.

Schreieder wanted to crush *Orde Dienst* completely, for there was a very real danger. If the British should succeed in their turn in duping Giskes and in providing the Resistance with weapons, then all hell would break loose. It would be as in France and Yugoslavia, with well-armed groups attacking the German forces. The relative peace maintained in Holland by Rauter and his underlings, through bloody repressions, would come to an end.

It was back in the summer of 1942 that Schreieder had decided he had enough codes, security checks and information of various kinds obtained from captured agents to launch an operation of his own, without saying a word about it to Major Giskes. And he sent for Van der Waals.

Antonius had changed. He now looked the *Kriminalrat* straight in the eye. Some of the money he had received for his dirty work had gone on buying loud clothes which gave him the appearance of a prosperous pimp. Schreieder much preferred the Van der Waals of the early days, when his scared look helped him to pass as a man being hunted by the police. The *Kriminalrat* handed him a file with the name 'D'Aquin' in thick black letters on the cover. Antonius looked through the contents while Schreieder explained the job in hand.

'I'm not asking you to arrest this man. Any traffic cop could do that. What I want is his whole group. The whole lot of them!' He corrected himself. 'All the leaders, anyway. But I warn you – they're very different from the innocents you've been handing over to me until now. D'Aquin is a career policeman, naturally distrustful. A mistake on your part, however slight, and his suspicions will be aroused. He's a man who'd shoot you without any hesitation.'

Schreieder was deliberately trying to frighten Van der Waals, knowing that he worked much better when anxious for his own skin. And he had already lost some of his jovial assurance. His hands were shaking a little as he put down the file.

'It's probably the most important job in your career,' added Schreieder. 'And you're the only person capable of pulling it off.'

This was not just flattery. Antonius got the message – if the affair was successful, it would be worth around three thousand guilders to him. That was all he saw in it, and that alone sustained him.

He made some notes from the reports in the file – D'Aquin's description, his age and habits – and studied a photograph of the man. He also copied a telephone number at The Hague which, said Schreieder, might be a way of contacting D'Aquin.

'I'll see what I can do,' he said, closing the file and standing up.

'As a final word,' said Schreieder, 'I won't give you any advice, but it would be better for this job if you changed your clothes. . . .'

Antonius glanced down at himself and reddened. 'Of course,' he muttered. 'Yes, of course.'

Antonius spent the next few days thinking of his method of approach. At the same time he was preparing the part to play. He let his beard grow, got out an old, dark suit and a shirt with a frayed collar. He was naturally very thin, so had no difficulty in appearing half-starved.

For two whole days he remained in his Amsterdam apartment, neglecting to wash and eating very little. When he went out, he looked the part. The date was 10 July 1942.

The first time he called the 'phone number provided by Schreieder there was no reply. He decided to try again before seeking another means of approach.

The second time, in the evening, someone answered at once, a man with a firm, educated voice. Antonius calmly explained that he had no idea what name to ask for, that the number had been given to him by a friend, he was at the end of his tether, he couldn't say any more. 'I'd like to meet you – as soon as possible.'

The other did not reply at once. Antonius could no longer hear the sounds in the background. The man must have put a hand over the receiver while consulting with someone else. After a minute or so, Antonius heard another, sharper voice say to him : 'Be at the entrance to the Passage, by the Binnenhoff, in an hour's time.' Then the man hung up.

It was insane! He had been given a rendezvous right opposite the Gestapo offices! Right in the lion's den. Van der Waals wondered whether he had been speaking to D'Aquin himself or to one of his lieutenants.

The Passage is, even now, a dreary shopping arcade. At that time, when the shops had very little to show, it was indeed gloomy and depressing. A few people still strolled along it, and tramps and poor Jews gathered round the heating ventilators. But the police very rarely put foot in this draughty haven. Actually, it was not a bad idea of D'Aquin (or whoever it was) to have fixed the rendezvous there.

Two men came, two tall men wearing grey raincoats. One was bareheaded, the other had a hat crammed down over his eyes. They walked straight up to Van der Waals. Neither was like the photo of D'Aquin that he had studied in the file. The taller of the two took Van der Waals firmly by the arm as though arresting him (and in fact he had the ridiculous idea that he was being arrested).

'Let's walk on a bit,' said the other.

They went down the arcade. 'Who are you?' asked the taller. Antonius gathered his thoughts, hesitated a moment, then took the plunge.

'I am a SOE agent, name is Jan, I was dropped near Dordrecht a fortnight ago. My radio operator was killed on landing. I'm cut off from everything. I must get in touch with London. It's urgent. I can't tell you why, but it's most important.'

It was an excellent performance – the voice gasping, halting, the words interspersed with nervous gulps, while searching for what he wanted to say next like a man whose brain was deadened by fatigue and hunger.

'We can't do anything for you,' the taller of the two said simply. 'We have no contact with England. We're as cut off as you are, my poor friend.'

In three short sentences he had admitted being engaged in the underground struggle and had revealed the tragic isolation of the Resistance. His companion was looking at him sternly. Why say so much to a stranger?

'Who gave you this telephone number?' the other said sharply to Van der Waals.

He had his reply to that all ready. 'A man in Dordrecht, but I don't know anything about him.'

'What's he like?'

'Fairly tall, with light ginger hair. I think he's a farmer.' (There was such a man. Schreieder had arrested him unobtrusively two days before, and he had admitted belonging to *Orde Dienst*.)

The three sauntered along, Van der Waals in the middle. This was not a case of arresting an infant or an agent who had lost his bearings. Van der Waals was up against something new and wondered what would happen next. He was frightened. The two rained questions at him, questions that were unconnected but had all to do with SOE and the Free Dutch. They were trying to get Antonius to contradict himself, the poor fellows! If they had known how much better informed he was on these subjects, and for what reasons. . . .

They apparently decided after a time that 'Jan' had passed his test. As for 'Jan', he kept saying, 'All I want is to warn London. All I ask you to do is to find me a radio operator with a transmitter, nothing else.'

'We'll see what we can do,' said the taller.

They arranged to meet him on the Maurits Kade in four days' time, and strode away into the crowd.

'So far so good,' Schreieder said to Van der Waals when he reported. 'And now, don't go and do something foolish, as you usually do.' Schreieder liked to humble Van der Waals, especially when he was frightened.

Van der Waals spent the next four days wandering about The Hague, knocking at doors that he knew would not be opened. They were the homes of Resistance members who had been arrested, some of them through his efforts. If he were being watched, these attempts being made by a hunted man would satisfy D'Aquin of his good faith.

He was at the Maurits Kade a little before time, and walked up and down with bowed head and his hands clasped behind his back, looking for all the world like a grief-stricken widower visiting a cemetery. The two Resistance men soon appeared. They hurried up to him, seized him by the arms even more firmly than at the first meeting, hauled him away from the quayside and bundled him into a small car of French make which was driven off in a north-westerly direction. They did not kill him. He was taken, blindfolded, to a country house which smelt of polish and gin. When the bandage was removed, Van der Waals found himself sitting opposite a small but broad-shouldered man wearing a double-breasted suit and tie. The light from a naked bulb shone straight into Antonius's eyes, and he blinked as he heard the man say, 'I may as well tell you at once – I don't like your ugly mug.'

This was D'Aquin. Antonius noticed the habit common to all policemen of emphasising vulgar words unnecessarily. He went on: 'But that's of no importance. You have to prove to us that you're a British agent. If you don't . . .' He made a quick gesture.

Antonius looked round at the other men silently standing there, steely-faced, neatly-dressed men, as in gangster films. D'Aquin seemed to have chosen his staff from the senior ranks of the Dutch police. Antonius realised it would be a waste of time to parley, to talk the matter over. He said in a simple, plain manner, without any aggressiveness: 'I think you've got an ugly mug too. Believe it or not, I had a different idea of the Resistance. However, I've no choice. I've a mission to carry out. I need your help, and that's all there is to it. As for the proof you ask for – I can give that all right. At eight o'clock tomorrow evening, Radio Oranje will broadcast the message 'The table is round.' Will that do?'

Antonius had been told about this code message by Schreieder. It was intended for a Resistance group which had been wiped out some time ago, but whose existence was being artificially maintained by the 'English Game'. London had been communicating with ghosts for weeks past. D'Aquin, of course, knew nothing of this.

'And what does this message mean?' he asked.

'It means they're expecting a report from me. They've been waiting for some time.'

'We'll see,' said D'Aquin.

The message was in fact no more than a routine signal, merely intended to maintain contact, and there was no certainty that it would be broadcast in the BBC 'Radio Oranje' programme on that particular day. Van der Waals was risking his life, and Schreieder had not concealed this from him.

'Of course, the message might not be broadcast for two or three days,' added 'Jan'. 'There's always that possibility.'

This hedging did not please D'Aquin. 'We'll see,' he repeated shortly.

He had as much need of 'Jan' as 'Jan' had of him. He longed to break the silence, to make contact with London, and 'Jan' provided him with a wonderful opportunity. But the agent's appearance was certainly not to his liking. He'd better wait and see. Van der Waals was blindfolded again, and the same car took him back to the centre of The Hague.

The following day he was waiting on the Maurits Kade again, at the same time. D'Aquin's two lieutenants came along and the same procedure took place as before. The scene in the living-room of the country house looked the same. D'Aquin and the others might never have budged from their positions. But D'Aquin seemed more relaxed. He handed round cigarettes and glasses of schnaps, and Antonius could not refuse. They talked of this and that while waiting for the broadcast. At eight o'clock D'Aquin switched on the radio and tuned in to the BBC 'Radio Oranje' programme.

At eight-thirty, Radio Oranje confirmed that the table was round.

'I believe you,' said D'Aquin. 'I can't do anything else.'

In the small living-room, which the owner (an old lady, almost certainly) had littered with spun-glass ornaments, there were five men all smoking and looking at Van der Waals. When they had recovered from their emotion, one of the five said, 'What's the next thing to do?' It was then that D'Aquin – fifteen years in the detective force, two years in counter-espionage and two years working underground – took a risk.

'If you like,' he said to 'Jan', 'you can be the radio operator of our group.' The others nodded approval. They showed little enthusiasm, but they approved.

Van der Waals was taken to his new lodgings – a room in the centre of the town. He was given some clean clothes, a little money and some food. Before leaving him, D'Aquin released what remained of his distrust in a scornful phrase. 'Eat and get some sleep. We'll come and fetch you early in the morning. Have a good wash too. Perhaps you'll look a lot better when you're clean.'

They were back at dawn, woke him up and took him in the car to the country house, without blindfolding him this time. D'Aquin was waiting there in his shirt sleeves. No one in the car had noticed that it was being followed by a laundry van. There was no laundry in the van, but lots of cable and wireless equipment and two men wearing headphones; it was Schreieder's radio van. It drew up in the village, about one hundred yards from the house. Later in the day, plain-clothed policemen took up positions in an empty house and watched the comings and goings at D'Aquin's house through binoculars.

An electrician belonging to D'Aquin's group had succeeded in putting together a transmitter-receiver, and this was already installed at the house. 'Jan' gave D'Aquin his code and told him the scheduled time for his transmission, 18.00 hours. Van der Waals had not invented anything. The code was that of a real agent, the radio operator of the 'Marrow' mission, and the transmission time had been fixed by Schreieder, whose specialists in the laundry van were preparing to 'play at being London'.

It had been decided that Van der Waals should operate the set, although he was not very good at it. He tuned in, and at six o'clock exactly he made contact with 'the British'. They were only a hundred yards away, as he well knew. It was a horrible farce which, if all went well, was bound to end with at least a score of men being sent to their deaths.

And all did go well. 'London' replied almost at once and very distinctly. 'Jan' began tapping out some items of information, all quite correct and which would have been very useful to the British, had they but received them. He gave the names and strength of the German divisions stationed in Holland and similar details about the *Luftwaffe* squadrons. Then, without a break in transmission, he asked for weapons, clothing and explosives to be dropped 'so that we can go into action as quickly as possible'.

'London' replied that an important parachute drop would be made on 21 July. The agent 'Jan' was to choose the dropping zone. And he was to be in sole charge of the operation.

The British were not in the habit of sending arms and ammunition by return, as it were, especially when an agent reported from the field for the first time. The decision was taken at a high level and after considerable thought. D'Aquin ought to have twigged this . . . but he knew nothing whatever about the British organisation. Although an active Resistant for two years, he had never received a sign of encouragement from the free world. He had never been present at a parachute drop. And he was in almost complete ignorance of the British attitude to subversive warfare.

So D'Aquin did not twig. On the contrary, when the transmission had ended, he and his staff made the effort to smile at 'Jan'.

'I knew it,' said D'Aquin jokingly. 'When you've had a wash, you're a much nicer person.' It was difficult for him to hide his feelings at having emerged at last from oblivion. There was much human warmth in that room just then – while a hundred yards away Schreieder's 'laundrymen' were re-winding their recording tapes.

Schreieder decided to act swiftly. With men like that, who could become dangerous at any moment, there was no time to lose!

'I need about twenty men,' said 'Jan'.

D'Aquin made a face. 'As many as that? There's only a dozen of us altogether.' He had to make a great effort to talk as a subordinate to this fellow who had been picked up in the street less than a week ago. But he had no choice. It was he himself who had made 'Jan' his link with London.

'It'll be quite a big parachute drop,' said 'Jan' with assurance. 'Twelve men are barely enough. Still.'

They separated, and 'Jan' was taken back to town in the small French car. It had been arranged that all would meet again between nine and ten on the evening of 20 July at the address given by 'Jan' – a house in a village about twenty-five miles from Utrecht. 'Arrive one at a time,' he had advised them. 'And in the meantime try to get hold of a van for carrying away all the material.'

At half-past nine on the evening of 20 July D'Aquin was walking alone down the village street. He came to the house and hesitated before ringing the bell. 'After all,' he thought, 'I don't know anything about this Jan. I ought to have questioned him more closely.' However, he gave three short rings as arranged. The door was opened almost immediately, but by a man who was a stranger to D'Aquin. He stepped back, a hand in his coat pocket.

'Isn't Jan here?' he asked, pointing his revolver inside his pocket.

'Yes,' said the man, all smiles. 'Yes, he's waiting for you.'

'Who are you?'

'A friend of Jan's. Come in, quick!'

D'Aquin stepped inside feeling suspicious, but he went in. The corridor was in darkness. The man went ahead, shining his torch on the floor like a cinema usherette. At the foot of the stairs he turned. 'They're up on the first floor. Mind how you go – the stairs are steep.'

D'Aquin followed him up. 'The others have arrived then?' D'Aquin asked.

'Some of them. Not all.'

The two reached a narrow landing and the man pushed open a door for D'Aquin to enter. He saw six of his comrades in a large, white-painted room. There were only three chairs, so three men were sitting on the floor. They were all handcuffed.

'I've been waiting for you impatiently,' Schreieder said to him.

All twelve were captured in exactly the same manner. Those not of great importance were brutally tortured. They talked, and other fighters in the shadows, other leaders, fell into Schreieder's net. Among them was a senior army officer, General Roell. The total number of arrests amounted to fifty. Van der Waals had well earned his three thousand guilders!

When Major Giskes heard about the arrests he arranged to meet the *Kriminalrat* at their usual place, the Red Lion Hotel in Amsterdam.

'I'm very satisfied,' Giskes said to the 'criminologist'. 'Satisfied at not being mixed up in this dirty business.'

D'Aquin, Roell and forty of their Resistance comrades were sentenced to death. Seyss-Inquart commuted the sentences passed on D'Aquin and Roell (the latter through the personal intervention of Hermann Goering!). But all the others were shot.

There remained the ideological Resistance, headed by a great political figure, a bearded Socialist leader with something of the aura of Léon Blum and who was president of the National Committee (a National Council of Resistance set up by several political parties). This man was Koos Vorrink, a past Prime Minister. Schreieder would have achieved little while Vorrink and his chief assistants were still at liberty. Vorrink had the gift of stirring men to action. During the pre-war years he had electrified crowds with speeches of great lyrical power. In 1942 he was little more than a symbol, but while he remained at liberty he could become a rally-ing-point for all the army in the shadows if the British succeeded in dropping quantities of arms and ammunition. Queen Wilhelmina had sent envoys on several occasions to persuade Vorrink to escape to London (the Queen wanted him to be Prime Minister of the Dutch Government in exile), but each time he had refused. 'My place is with the Dutch people,' he had said.

For the moment, his only weapon was the printed word. The National Committee printed and distributed a great number of clandestine leaflets – declarations of policy, manifestos, calls for a general strike – which bore the unmistakable stamp of Vorrink's eloquent prose style.

This head of a weaponless army, the prisoner of a committee which was not always in agreement with him, could do little else but clench his fists. Schreieder knew through his V-men that Vorrink wanted desperately to contact London, to be able to tell the world of his country's long agony. For the second time, the *England Spiel* was about to assist the repressive measures of the Germans.

By November 1942, Schreieder was in possession of much more information concerning Vorrink and his organisation than he had ever had about D'Aquin. The file that the *Kriminalrat* handed to Van der Waals was bulging between the covers. The latter knew what Vorrink looked like, having seen his photo in the papers almost daily before the war. Vorrink was considered an idealist, rather ingenuous, but Schreieder warned Antonius not to rely on this. Then he produced part of a cracked photograph showing a small girl posing solemnly in a kitchen garden.

'The other part is in the possession of a man called Wims,' Schreieder explained. 'You're to find him and show him this part as your credentials. Then you'll follow him. If he doesn't kill you straight away, he'll lead you to Vorrink.' Antonius was becoming used to Schreieder's peculiar sense of humour, so he smiled. They spent the evening laying their plans.

Van der Waals was to play the part of an agent from London once again. But this time he would not be a lone worker in search of a haven and a transmitter. He would be on a definite mission, accumulating arms and explosives for concerted subversive action by several Resistance groups.

Wims was one of Vorrink's lieutenants. He was in possession

of weapons and a quantity of explosives, and was expecting to receive orders from London through an agent (who had been captured three weeks ago). Antonius would go to collect the weapons and explosives, and talk about his radio contacts with London. He would ask to meet Vorrink in order to put these contacts at his disposal.

The scenario had much in common with that for the D'Aquin affair. But Schreieder decided that his next victim would actually exchange messages with London, instead of with laundrymen in a van parked at the corner of the street. He and Giskes controlled enough radio links to play this game. Besides, Schreieder was aiming at more than the capture of Vorrink and the members of the National Committee. He thought that London might give Vorrink important details of Allied strategy. The *Kriminalrat* even hoped that, through Vorrink, he might learn the date and place of the Invasion. . . .

Antonius met Wims on 1 December 1942, and everything went off as expected. Wims copied his leaders' sayings and their drooping shoulders. His face shone with the high idea he had of responsibility, and his frank look brightened his terribly thin features. He was waiting for Antonius, alias De Wilde, in a certain room in Amsterdam. Antonius produced his torn photograph, and Wims showed him the other part.

'That's fine,' said Wims. 'You can collect the stuff this evening. I leave it to you to find transport, that's none of my business. I don't want to know about it. I just do my job, that's all. Just do my job.'

He repeated himself as children do when playing at being grown-ups, to seem more mature. Antonius reached for one of the rush-bottom chairs, turned it round and sat astride it with his arms resting on the back, facing him. 'You've got nothing to ask me?' he said, puckering up his brow.

'What is there to ask?' Wims replied with a shrug. 'You've shown me the photo, you're going to take the stuff away. That's fine, there's no need for anything else. The less one knows, the better, especially in our job.'

He was pathetic, with his hardened way of speaking. Antonius opened up. 'Suppose I haven't come just to collect the 'stuff'. Suppose – I've a radio link with London.'

'I don't want to know about it. I've told you.'

'Listen a minute,' Antonius insisted. 'I know your National Committee needs to have a radio contact with the British. And the British are eager to know what's happening here.'

Wims waved his words aside, saying 'It's nothing to do with me, not my concern.' But Antonius saw that his face was reddening.

'We'll talk about it later,' said 'De Wilde', standing up. 'See you tomorrow, same time.'

Wims did not say no.

Next day, Antonius arrived dead on time. (During the night, some men under his orders had removed the 'stuff' – a hundred Stens and eighty pounds of explosives – which went to increase the stocks of weapons and explosives seized as a result of Operation North Pole.)

'Take a seat and listen,' said Wims. 'I've had a word with the chief. He'd like to see you. But mind! He's a big shot and no fool. He'll see at once if you're bluffing. And if you are . . .' He made the same quick gesture as D'Aquin had on first meeting Van der Waals. (Very likely Van Looi did not like his ugly mug either.)

That evening Wims took him to a disused building in the southern outskirts of Amsterdam. He did not think it necessary to blindfold 'De Wilde', or even to take him by a roundabout route, thus showing that he had no doubts about him. In a room at the back, six men were sitting round a table on a raised platform. The flickering light from a carbide lamp made the shadows dance on their faces. Van der Waals recognised one of them as Koos Vorrink, despite the pointed beard he now wore and which gave him the appearance of a young mandarin. Besides, he made no mystery about it. He came down from the platform and held out his hand.

'Vorrink, president of the National Committee.'

His grasp squeezed Wims' limp fingers. An historic encounter of courage and fear, of idealism and treachery.

'I hear that you've come to help us,' said Vorrink.

His words rang true and he made no attempt to conceal his pleasure. Wims had withdrawn to his place among the watchers near the door.

'Of course,' added Vorrink, stern of a sudden, 'you can prove that you've been sent by London?'

Antonius replied that nothing was simpler. Mr President had only to listen to Radio Oranje in two days' time. It was the same trick as had succeeded so well with D'Aquin. And he had been much more suspicious than was Vorrink, so there was nothing to fear on that score.

Vorrink gave 'De Wilde' another firm, frank handshake before he left. Vorrink did not have him followed, but even if he had he would not have discovered his connection with the Gestapo. Antonius went straight home and telephoned to Schreieder from there. Then slept soundly.

Vorrink was wild with hope. The day before, about four hundred and fifty Jewish men, women and children had been packed into a train and taken to Westerborck concentration camp. Vorrink had seen these hapless people sitting on their suitcases outside the railway station, which was cordoned off by German soldiers. They were awaiting their departure for Death with heartrending apathy. Children were stroking the dogs set to guard them. Were it not for the soldiers and the yellow stars sewn on the Jews' coats, one would have taken them for a crowd going on holiday.

'The people in London certainly don't know about the deportations, the torturing and the killings!' exclaimed Vorrink. 'They must be told, and quickly!'

Van der Waals listened and said nothing. Radio Oranje had duly provided him with credentials. Vorrink had heard the code message with his own ears. He and 'De Wilde' had arranged that the latter would take the messages and transmit them to London, then bring the replies to Vorrink. Antonius had said he was very sorry but he could on no account reveal where he transmitted from or give any details. Vorrink had not protested. In fact he had said afterwards, according to Wims: 'I'm all in favour of keeping things apart. The less we know about one another's work, the better.' There were no difficulties in that respect. Antonius was able to do his dirty work in all privacy.

But the first message that Vorrink gave to him was a long proclamation beginning, 'Are you in agreement with the creation of a National Committee?' This was followed by a political manifesto interspersed with descriptions of the maryrdom of Holland.

Schreieder could not avoid calling on Giskes for the help of his radio room in order to transmit Vorrink's messages to London. But the shoe pinched. When Giskes (who already took a dim view of the operation) read the first message he almost jumped from his chair. He sent it, just the same. This was not the moment to fall out with the Gestapo. But he firmly asked Schreieder to 'put an end to this stupid business which could completely compromise the *England Spiel*'. The British were hungry for information of tactical importance and had no wish for political manifestos!

London's reply to the first message (sent on Christmas Eve, 1942) was simply 'Cut it short.'

Van der Waals took the reply to Vorrink, a political orator who had strayed into secret warfare where silence was the rule. Vorrink frowned, made some cuts in his text, but continued composing messages on the same subjects.

Giskes became exasperated. London was irritated. The British were receiving appeals choked with indignation. Vorrink informed them of the composition of his government for after the war, sent long memoranda about the political and economic situation. He also asked for arms, but did not say when, where or how he would collect them. It was incredible that Vorrink, who counted the number of massacres, should never have thought of descending from the clouds to take part in some active measures.

'After sending the fifth message,' wrote Giskes, 'we were requested by London to put an end to this foolery. It was of no interest and needlessly exposed the operator to risk of detection. Nevertheless, we continued until January (1943), but the sole result was a message for Vorrink from London which showed no enthusiasm whatever for his projects. . . .'[1]

As the days passed, or rather the nights, Van der Waals continued carrying the messages to and fro between Schreieder and Vorrink. Although deeply hurt by the British replies, the president of the National Committee still sent his manifestos and proclamations. He was unaware, of course, that they were edited by Giskes and Schreieder, who gave them a little interest by adding items of information – false, naturally.

This was the time when Giskes and Schreieder reached the

[1] *op. cit.*

summit of their *England Spiel*, that Everest of counter-intelligence. From now on, they had to descend, the more difficult part.

The situation was complicated even more by Van der Waals, who was getting bored with being just a messenger boy and started making blunders. He was wearing his loud suits again and throwing his money about. While the Resistance men, Vorrink and his colleagues, were going hungry, 'De Wilde' always looked well-fed. And he went to night clubs frequented by German soldiers, places where a Resistance man had no business to be. He also began to boast that he was a nephew of Prime Minister Gerbrandy. A young Resistance fighter named Tijn, who had been watching him closely for some time, realised the part he was playing. Tijn was about to report his misgivings to the National Committee when, fortunately for Schreieder, he was arrested.

As though this were not enough, Vorrink added to Schreieder's difficulties by deciding to have his own direct radio link with London. (What reason was there for refusing him?) Vorrink had found a radio operator, Van Looi, a man of disarming frankness who had brought his civil servant's manners into underground warfare.

This was in early February 1943. Van der Waals provided the set for the National Committee's own radio post, but it was tuned in to Giskes's office. The same trick was being employed as with D'Aquin, but eliminating the laundrymen; and instead of Schreieder replying, Vorrink's messages were transmitted to London by Giskes, in carefully edited versions, and London's replies were first received by Giskes and then relayed to Van Looi's receiver. Giskes was becoming increasingly irritated by the whole business, predicting that no good would come of it.

Then, on 8 March, Van Looi's petty bureaucratic scruples came to the surface. He put his own spoke into the exchanges between the National Committee and London, which were already confused enough, edited by the Gestapo and heavily overloaded. On his own initiative he tapped out this message:

'Quite willing to work for the military stop am making war in all possible ways stop but refuse to be franc tireur stop army rank too low stop wish to be officially appointed stop Van Looi message ends.'

By signing his message he gave the final touch to this horrible farce whereby a Gestapo chief was transmitting to London reports on the situation of Jews in Holland (deportations, description of Westerborck concentration camp, etc.) and presenting the future of the Dutch Social Democratic Party!

Schreieder had had enough of it. He first calmed Van Looi by sending him the message: 'Van Looi given rank of lieutenant for duration of hostilities.' The poor man was not to enjoy his promotion for long.

On 10 March 1943, Vorrink, his brother Louis and Van der Waals were walking along one of the quays at The Hague, their coat-collars turned up against the rain. Van der Waals seemed as much taken by surprise as the other two when a squad of leather-coated Dutchmen suddenly pounced on them. The evening before, Vorrink had said, 'They'll never capture me. I'd rather kill myself first.' But he was not given the time. They grasped his arms and twisted his wrists and forced him into a strait-jacket, as were the other two, Antonius included. The passers-by thought that a few escaped maniacs were being captured. Vorrink was gagged before he could give a shout. By the following day, practically all the members of the National Committee were in prison.

It was then that Major Giskes told the *Kriminalrat* just what he thought of him.

'My dear chap,' said Giskes, 'you've just made the second serious mistake in the *England Spiel*. The first was to infiltrate your scum into the National Committee. We could have easily helped Vorrink to exchange messages with London, without showing our hand. The second mistake was to arrest Vorrink. I had need of him myself. And do you know why? I'll tell you. Because we shall never find another leader of the Resistance as docile as he was. There was every advantage in letting him remain at liberty. He would never have succeeded in grouping all the Resistance behind him. He was too much of a dreamer for that. On the other hand, there was always the possibility that the British would have given him some important mission, and eventually the date of the Invasion. As a prisoner, perhaps a dead one by tomorrow, he becomes a national hero. His importance greatly increases. His corpse could become a symbol for the Resistance fighters. Finally, when the British learn of his arrest, they'll become more suspicious. They'll almost certainly investigate and tighten things up. And that'll be the end of the *England Spiel*! That's what I wanted to say to you, mister policeman!'

This scene took place in Giskes's office. Both men were standing, Giskes tall and upright, Schreieder with his little brown-button eyes, furious with rage, on a level with the major's Iron Cross.

Schreieder did not argue. He contented himself with saying that Vorrink's arrest and the duping of the National Committee were police matters, a field that was no concern of the major's. And he went out slamming the door behind him. (Sooner or later he would have the last word, for he knew from highly-placed sources that the Himmler organisation was going to take over the *Abwehr*, like an industrial combine absorbing a small firm.) Schreieder was dreaming of his revenge.

As for Vorrink, the German authorities did worse than killing him by not bringing him to trial, by treating him well and leaving him to form Socialist committees among his fellow prisoners! Vorrink was to survive the war and emerge from prison broken in health and politically discredited.

Giskes was wrong on another point – the arrest of the National Committee did not bring about the demise of the *England Spiel*. Presumably the British, relieved by the Germans of a correspondent who was something of a nuisance, were not led to the conclusion that all the Resistance groups in Holland had either been wiped out or were penetrated by the enemy. And yet that, alas, was the situation in the early part of 1943. Except for the Communists and a few small, isolated groups, the Dutch secret army had ceased to exist.

But the *England Spiel* was bound to come to an end. The British would eventually understand, one way or another. The great question in March 1943 was, who would break up the 'English Game'?

How? And at what cost?

PART THREE *The Ending*

13

The Tables Begin to Turn

Pieter Dourlein was swayed slightly in the cold night air. Dourlein had seen much fighting in many parts of the world. Less than a week after being released with a clean bill from the Patriotic School he had joined the Dutch cruiser *Isaac Swers*. During the next twelve months he had left the ship only for a few brief but memorable shore-leaves at Gibraltar, Cape Town and Glasgow. He had sailed in Malta convoys, fought the Germans in the Atlantic and the Japanese in the Far East, winning several medals and acquiring a good knowledge of English.

When on leave in London, while his ship was being repaired at Southampton, he volunteered for 'Special Work'. From September 1942 to February 1943 the British had trained him, disciplined and toughened him. And now, on the night of 3 March 1943, he was dangling from a parachute. His pals, Bogaart and Arense, had jumped just before him. They must be floating down somewhere below. He could not see them. Probably they had already landed.

Dourlein was a good man – sentimental, yet a tough young fighter. There were tears in his eyes just now. Only a few hundred feet below him was the Dutch earth, which he had not seen or smelt for nearly two years. He was returning as a hero, as an avenging angel with parachute harness cutting into his armpits, a German revolver digging into his side and a whole lot of equipment hampering his movements.

Waiting for him below were unknown compatriots who had faced death a thousand times. He, Bogaart and Arense, had come to help them (Bogaart was a radio operator, Arense and Dourlein were saboteurs). They were the 'Sprout' mission, with orders to join the Resistance fighters (Dourlein had been told in England that they were very numerous, not too well off for leaders but with high morale and all stout-hearted) and to give technical training to certain groups. But the mission's most important task was to establish a new radio link between the Resistance and London.

Dourlein suddenly saw little white lights winking below him, a little to the right. They grew rapidly bigger, and he then realised that he was falling very quickly. The inky darkness below him had turned to dark brown, and he could make out the evenly-spaced, straight lines of a freshly ploughed field. Five seconds later, he touched the ground. There was no wind, and the parachute fell around him like a shroud. As he was struggling to free himself, Dourlein heard cheerful Dutch voices welcoming him and asking whether he was hurt. When his head emerged from the parachute he saw three young men in leather jackets smiling at him in the light of their torches. One of them handed him a mug of hot, sweet coffee.

They gathered up his scattered equipment, buried his parachute in the twinkling of an eye, and led him behind a hedge where Boogaart and Arendse were waiting for him. But his two comrades had not a word to say; they were gagged. Before Dourlein could recover from his surprise, one of the men (probably Den Droog) snapped handcuffs on him. Dourlein yelled and kicked out. Handcuffed though he was, he tried to get at his revolver, but one of the traitors knocked him out with a powerful blow to the chin.

Daybreak found him where so many of his comrades had been before him – in the Gestapo offices at The Hague. Dourlein, who had previously been fighting a war that was bloody but downright, in which the good Allies fought the dirty enemy, was now brought face to face with a different reality. There existed traitors, despicable cowards, double agents. He had been betrayed – by whom? His head was still aching from the blow, and this kind of question was beyond him for the moment. Nobody in England had told him anything about this.

Inspector Bayer had laid out on the table the few things found on Dourlein – the revolver, a forged identity card, a box of matches. With this small display, Bayer was going to break Pieter's morale. It was so easy! He took the matchbox between his fat thumb and forefinger and held it up to Dourlein, who was chained by his handcuffs to the hot-water pipes. Bayer looked for all the world like a conjuror about to perform one of his best tricks, and he spoke to Pieter as though addressing the good folk at a church fête.

'You see this box? Well, I'm going to tell you what it contains. You and these gentlemen here' (he nodded towards the Gestapo men in the room) 'can bear witness that I haven't opened it. Inside this box is a cigarette paper.' He then opened the box, broke the false bottom and drew out a tightly-rolled tube of paper about the size of a toothpick. 'You see? All your comrades had the same thing! And now listen carefully. Without unrolling this paper, I'll tell you what is written on it. All the stages of your escape route are written on it! That's right, isn't it?' (Dourlein clenched his teeth, and his big jaws shook.) 'If you happened to part company with us, you would go straight to Rotterdam, to Rochussenstraat. Am I right?'

He was right. But Dourlein would never admit it, not even under a thousand blows.

Bayer did not content himself with this one telling blow. He bludgeoned Dourlein with the names of the fifteen people and the addresses of their 'safe houses' in Belgium, France and Switzerland, that Dourlein had spent two days learning by heart.

'We know everything, absolutely everything, about you and your organisation. Your immediate superior is Captain Lieftinck.' (Lieftinck, who had stood them a round of drinks just before they left!) 'Bingham, an Englishman, is in charge of your training.' (True!) 'Major Gubbins plans your missions.' (True!) 'I could go on for hours. I tell you, Mr Dourlein, we know everything.'

It was like a horrible nightmare. And Dourlein knew that he would not easily wrench himself out of it. But Bayer had not yet broken any vital part of his morale. He was tired, but not prostrate. At that moment he was fuming because he had been captured without a fight, because he had not put up more of a fight. His actual interrogation was very short. Bayer put a few questions about detail, but which elicited no reply from Dourlein. He was not tortured. Bayer dared not allow it, as he did not know whether the man was important and whether Giskes and Schreieder intended to use him. However, although Dourlein was not tortured physically, Inspector Bayer could not resist the pleasure of showing him his comrades who were already in the Gestapo prison.

Dourlein was bound hand and foot. He made no resistance, realising it was useless. He was laid on a stretcher, and the stretcher was put into an army ambulance. Just before midday the ambulance drove into the courtyard of Haaren prison, the stretcher was taken out and Dourlein was untied (he still knew nothing of what had happened to Boogaart and Arendse). When he stood up, he felt a revolver pressed in his back. It was held by Bayer.

'Whatever you see here,' said the inspector, 'keep silent. If you make a sound, if you utter a single word, I warn you – I shall shoot.'

Dourlein was saving his rebellious actions for later. He nodded, and for a split second Bayer saw the nape of his neck, as though ready for the bullet. They climbed the new steel staircase, one behind the other, with some Dutch jailers following at a distance. On the second floor, Bayer prodded Dourlein to walk along the corridor, past the cell doors, each of which now had a small steel shutter in place of the peephole.

Bayer, still holding his revolver in Dourlein's back, slid back one shutter a little way. 'Look in there!'

Dourlein put his left eye to the horizontal slit.

'D'you know him?'

Dourlein shook his head. (He had not said a word since his capture; it would not have been unreasonable of Bayer to have concluded that Dourlein did not understand German nor his bad Dutch.) The man in the cell was Takonis. Dourlein had never seen him before. He belonged to the early batch of sacrificed men. They passed on to the next cell. Dourlein did not know its occupant either. The man had probably been arrested before he himself was enrolled into SOE.

'What about this one?' asked Bayer, half opening a third shutter. This man was Van Os. Dourlein had done his training with him in various camps. Van Os had been parachuted in February. Dourlein opened his mouth, but immediately felt Bayer's breath on his neck.

'Not a sound! Don't forget – I'll shoot!'

Dourlein shrugged his shoulders. But Bayer had not finished. He showed Dourlein the haggard faces of Van den Bor, Bragger,

Van Hulsteyn, Kist and other agents he knew, some of whom were his pals. And on their ashen faces Dourlein read something worse than despair – resignation.

'You know them, don't you?' Bayer kept saying, getting more and more agitated.

When Dourlein had seen the last prisoner, sitting on his bench and gazing at his useless hands, he suddenly turned to Bayer and shouted loudly, 'Yes, I knew them all – once upon a time!'

Bayer did not shoot him. The inspector had made a grave mistake in thinking that Dourlein would sink to the depths of despair, as the others had done, when the absurdity of his mission had been so amply demonstrated. Bayer was never more mistaken. Dourlein was not a man to break down.

He was interrogated a little more in the following days. Bayer took the opportunity to show him that the Germans knew even more than he did about SOE, and that nothing of the British secret plans escaped them. But Dourlein maintained a stubborn silence. Nothing touched him – neither Bayer's sarcasm nor his 'revelations'. Dourlein heard all right, but he hardly listened, and his captors became secretly convinced that they had hold of someone out of the ordinary.

Finally Schreieder put in an appearance. He had been told that the agent Dourlein was by no means easy to deal with. The *Kriminalrat* parked himself solidly in front of Pieter, who looked at him with complete indifference.

'So you refuse to help us,' said Schreieder. 'All right!' He said no more, and went out slamming the door behind him. In the corridor he said to Bayer: 'Don't waste your time on him. He's no use to us, he's only a saboteur.' Pieter was taken back to Haaren and put in a new, white cell.

This was the Gestapo's second major mistake. It never occured to them that Dourlein, whole in body and mind, could still be dangerous even when shut up between four walls. He was just that much too obstinate to give in as the others had done. Hardly had the door closed on him than the pipes along the floor began to vibrate noisily. Dourlein had heard about the prisoners' telephone system. He put his ear to the lead pipes and heard a message in Morse: 'This is for the new arrivals ... What are your names....' Dourlein answered by tapping with his signet-ring (that he had been allowed to keep): 'Dourlein ... Bogaart

155

... Arense.' There was a short silence, then the pipe vibrated again. 'Welcome to you all.' Pieter replied: 'Thank you ... Who betrayed us. ... ?'

A fine old din broke out. The occupants of several cells were tapping on the pipes at the same time. Dourlein had the greatest difficulty in understanding, and in any case the names meant nothing to him. 'Lauwers ... Baatsen ... No, Jordaan was the traitor. ... That is a lie. ... Van der Reyden. ...' The tappings were sharp and hurried. They were no longer intended for Dourlein – the prisoners were abusing one another, giving vent to their feelings. Pieter wrapped his jacket round the pipe to muffle the sounds then tried to get some sleep. The situation was clear to him now: obviously his fellow-prisoners had been brain-washed and were beaten, and he had to escape as soon as possible.

'It's strange that none of them has tried to escape,' he thought before dropping off to sleep.

He was presuming too much, he did not know that none had tried to escape. And he was ignorant of the fact that Schreieder had found a simple but effective way of preventing any attempt to escape. The *Kriminalrat* had warned them all that if just one agent escaped, the rest would be shot at dawn the next day.

The SOE agents in Haaren prison were surprised and vaguely grateful at still being alive. Far from attempting anything, they hoped for nothing more than to be left as they were. Dourlein understood this clearly the following morning at exercise time, when the prisoners were allowed to talk.

He saw Bogaart again. At least, the slouching man he was walking behind had the appearance and answered to the name of Bogaart. But after only forty-eight hours as a prisoner and having probably undergone exhausting interrogations, the man was no longer Dourlein's old pal, the moving spirit and leader of the 'Sprout' mission. He, too, had succumbed to the arguments which had crushed the spirit of so many others. When Pieter asked him if he intended to try anything, he shrugged his shoulders and growled furiously that he was only too glad to be alive to risk his neck in some hopeless venture.

Pieter said no more. He got much the same reply from Arense. But one man on his own never makes a successful escape (so all the books say). He had to find an accomplice. But which, if any, of these burrowing insects, these flabby moles interned at Haaren was likely to work with him?

During the next week or two, Dourlein watched his fellow prisoners carefully and listened to their talk at exercise time. He did not find much ground for optimism. Not one of them seemed to have the guts or courage, or even any desire to escape. At the end of a month, Dourlein decided to postpone his attempt.

On 6 April 1943, a German officer was shot dead in the street at Breda. The Gestapo at once took forty leading townspeople as hostages and sent them to Haaren prison. A firing squad was preparing to shoot ten of them when the assassin was arrested. The hostages were released. Dourlein was returning from the infirmary when he met this group of men emerging from their terrible nightmare. Some of them were weeping with the sudden relief.

Dourlein was holding between his thumb and forefinger a paper pellet that he had been hiding for several days. It was pure chance that he should be out of his cell just when the hostages were being released. He had been taken to the infirmary for treatment to a boil. However, he seized the opportunity and picked out the man with the most trustworthy face. He was about forty, slightly better dressed than the others, and was holding a black hat with a curved brim. His name is said to have been Koersen, but this is far from certain.

Dourlein bumped into him. As he apologised he took the man's hand and shook it, pressing the paper pellet into his palm and whispering 'for the Resistance'. The man kept the paper, and without even a glance at Dourlein slowly nodded three times. Dourlein had written on the piece of paper: 'Whole SOE organisation in German hands, including radio posts. All agents captured. Dourlein.' Lauwers's messages had fallen on deaf ears. Had Dourlein's warning any better chance of not remaining a dead letter?

One morning in June, Dourlein's cell-door was opened and in came a reserved little man who looked as stubborn as a mule – as stubborn as Dourlein. The man threw his blankets on the iron bed that two jailers had brought in, and held out his hand to Dourlein.

'My name's Ubbink.'

'Mine's Dourlein.'

Ubbink had been dropped a few weeks previously and was captured by Schreieder's men just as Dourlein had been. His mind, too, was bent on escape and he was looking for an accomplice. Ubbink did not have Dourlein's strength, but he was handier. Both had learned a great deal from the technical instruction given by SOE. They started at once to draw up a plan.

Pieter had recalled something that an instructor at Reading had said: 'You don't realise at first glance, but the space between the bars of a cell window is often wide enough for a man to squeeze through.' Pieter measured the gap between the iron bars of the fan-window above the door, and saw that his head and shoulders could pass through. And he was the broader of the two men.

Their plan was simple, and quite mad. It consisted of squeezing through the fan-window above their door, dropping down into the corridor, dashing to one of the lavatories and shutting themselves in, getting through another fan-window to the outside, crawling along to the barbed-wire fence and getting through that. They needed the help of their fellow-prisoners, which would not be easy to get. Nevertheless, Dourlein and Ubbink encouraged each other and felt confident. They knew, or at least they hoped, that at the last minute the others would help them, even though their escape might bring reprisals.

At the end of June, they had a setback. They were separated. Ubbink was put in the next cell and two strangers joined Dourlein. They could now only communicate during excercise time and over the pipes. But Ubbink soon made a hole between their cells with a sharpened spoon. The scratching noise was covered by Baatsen, who was still singing excerpts from operas. So they were able to talk freely again. At the same time, their cell companions learned of their plan, and implored them to give it up.

'You're mad, you haven't a hope! You'll get a bullet in the back, not to mention that you're a couple of dirty bastards – the Boches will shoot some of the prisoners!'

Ubbink and Dourlein refused to listen. They knew that there was a lot of truth in what the others said, and they were afraid of being influenced by them. Occasionally Ubbink or Dourlein replied, 'Anyway, they'll kill all of us one day. If we're going to be bumped off, it might as well be in the open air.'

The two had judged the matter correctly. The others secretly envied them the courage which they themselves lacked, and when the time came they would give the necessary help.

At six in the evening on 23 July 1943, Dourlein and Ubbink began loosening the bars of the cell windows with makeshift files. By 15 August Dourlein had worked loose the bars of his fan-window. Two days later, Ubbink had done the same. The difficulty was to hold the bars in place, but they succeeded by using a mixture of breadcrumbs and plaster. Then they had to wait for a favourable opportunity. The prison seemed busier than ever; there was constant movement along the corridors and stairs by day and by night. Prisoners were always being transferred, others were brought in, and some were taken away to their deaths (either a lingering death in a concentration camp or a quick death by firing squad). The SOE agents, a special species in this penitentiary world, listened to all this activity and hunched their shoulders. Ubbink and Dourlein realised that it was not the time to make their attempt.

On 31 August, a Sunday, there was comparative calm in the prison. It was full, but no one was being taken away – as though most of the staff had gone on holiday. The quiet was broken only by a few shouts and the jailers making their rounds. At six that evening two jailers, one German and the other Dutch, came along the corridor pushing the supper trolley as usual. At each cell, the German opened the door and pushed the mess tins in with his foot, then slammed the door shut and locked it again. This clattering and clanging was very familiar to the prisoners, and they knew that nothing more would happen until the jailers came round at eight o'clock.

By seven minutes past six the trolley had reached the end of the corridor and the noise ceased. Dourlein and Ubbink were ready and waiting, each standing in his cell bare to the waist and counting up to fifty. One of Dourlein's cell-mates made a last appeal. 'You haven't got a chance – don't be a fool!' Nevertheless, he had promised to throw Dourlein's clothes through the fan-window after him.

Fifty! Each climbed on to the shoulders of a fellow prisoner, pushed the two loosened bars apart and squeezed through. Ubbink, who was the thinner, got through first. At ten past, Dourlein was through and found Ubbink waiting for him in the corridor. They picked up their clothes, which had been pushed through after them, dashed along to a lavatory and shut themselves in.

Eight o'clock came, and the jailer's last round of the day. He collected the prisoners' clothes (which were returned to them at six the following morning). He usually took the bundle handed to him without looking through it to see how many prisoners' clothes he was being given. If he stopped to count – ! But he continued along to the next cells without noticing anything amiss.

Midnight came at last. The two were only just beginning their escape. If caught now, they could put up a story. At midnight, the lights in the prison were switched off. Dourlein went through the fan-light first (the bars were a little wider apart than in their cells), and slid down a rope of knotted sheets. Less than a minute after he reached the ground, Ubbink was beside him. They pulled down the rope just before the moving searchlight passed across the window. They were outside, but not yet out of the prison. They still had to crawl across fifty yards of black mud to reach the barbed wire and the wall. It was pouring with rain. Half-past twelve. They were wet through and had crawled almost to the wire when the searchlight, passing over them, lit up a sentry. He halted just in front of them, and they dropped flat, holding their breath. In spite of the rain, the soldier remained there, standing at ease. His boots shone brightly, and he was a terrifying sight. But he was alone. Ubbink held Dourlein back from pouncing on him and strangling him as the instructor at Reading had taught them. It was better to wait.

They waited for a good fifteen minutes, motionless on the wet ground. Every sixty seconds the searchlight swept across the space just in front of them. At last the soldier moved. As though under the eye of his sergeant-major, he sprang to attention, clicked his heels, made a smart turn and marched away. Dourlein and Ubbink dashed for the fence with common accord – words were not necessary. The barbed wire was loose. They lifted it, and in a moment were over the wall and away. The street outside was deserted. They ran along it and took the first turn on the right, then the first on the left, then the first on the right again. They kept running, running. If the sea had not been in the way they would have gone on running all the way to London, and more in sorrow than in anger would have said to *them*: 'What the hell have you been doing to our friends?'

Kriminalrat Joseph Schreieder had promised Rauter, through Harster, that not one *England Spiel* agent would escape. In return, he had received the assurance that they would not be brought to trial while they continued to be of use to the operation. It followed that Major Giskes relied on Schreieder, in their common interest, to keep tight hold of the prisoners.

When Giskes's batman woke him at eight o'clock on 1 September with the news that two agents had escaped from Haaren, the major was quite unprepared for such a disaster. His mind was fixed on the technical problems of the *England Spiel*, and he had long stopped thinking about prison security. Besides, that was Schreieder's job, and Giskes thought that he could at least trust the *Kriminalrat* in that respect. So Giskes had a very rude awakening. He was at Haaren by eleven o'clock. The *Kriminalrat* was waiting for him, and had already taken disciplinary action. The prison commandant had been dismissed, the sentries were posted as 'volunteers' for the Russian front, and the prisoners were being deprived of their bread ration for a month, all as a 'preliminary' measure.

Schreieder, more talkative than ever, was telling Giskes of these decisions when the major was unable to contain his wrath any longer.

'That's not my affair,' he burst out, interrupting Schreieder. 'It's a matter for your police! All I want to say to you is this – if you don't recapture these two men, for whom, incidentally, I've every admiration, then the bottom will fall out of the *England Spiel*.'

Giskes added, touching the little Bavarian on the raw: 'And don't forget what you've often told me – that *you* are responsible for guarding the agents. It's in *your* interest to recapture them.' The *Abwehr* major had got some of his own back on the Gestapo policeman, who had often exasperated him with his 'My dear comrade, it's not your concern.' But this was poor consolation. Supposing Ubbink or Dourlein succeeded in reaching England, or simply contacted the Resistance and found a radio operator to report to London?

'I've taken all possible measures,' said Schreieder. 'The Dutch police, the *Feldgendarmerie* and the frontier guards have all been given a description of the two wanted men. I'm having posters printed, with their photos. A big reward will be offered for their capture.' Schreieder did all this and more. A whole army of police took part in the man hunt. Posters describing the two men were stuck up all over Holland, and the Germans offered five hundred guilders for information leading to their recapture. Road blocks were set up, and SS search parties with tracker dogs combed the countryside.

But neither Ubbink nor Dourlein was ever found.

14

The Massacre

Something had to be done, thought Major Giskes. He had little hope in his idea, but on 2 September he sent an urgent message to London over one of his controlled radio posts:

'Two Gestapo agents on way to England stop their names are Ubbink and Dourlein stop caution very dangerous stop pretending to be SOE agents stop should be arrested on arrival message ends.' It was not very clever, but was the only means he had of delaying the unmasking of the *England Spiel*. Otherwise, he had no illusions. He did not believe that Schreieder's police nor their dogs would find the two men who possessed the courage, audacity and determination to make such a successful escape. Giskes was expecting any day to receive a message from London saying – probably ironically – that the joke had lasted long enough.

However, dark clouds were gathering on another part of the horizon. Himmler's intrigues against Canaris were about to come to fruition. Giskes had been told by friends in Berlin that a bulky file on the *England Spiel* had been sent to Himmler, and that in it he, Giskes, was accused of intelligence with the enemy!

What were the difficulties of the *England Spiel* in comparison with the threats to the Third Reich? The Russians were sweeping into Poland, the Allies were slowly advancing up the boot of Italy. In Berlin, inevitably, defeatism was rearing its ugly head and purges were the order of the day. The SS chiefs blamed the reverses on the army leaders in general and the *Abwehr* specialists in particular.

However, contrary to all expectations, the 'English Game' was not yet over. Despite the escape of Ubbink and Dourlein, despite Lauwers's repeated warnings, the messages smuggled out of prison, and a hundred and one alarming signs, *they* were still carrying on! The British had not dropped any more agents into

Holland, it was true, after the three despatched on 22 May 1943 (Brey, Mink and Punt) but the exchange of radio messages continued. The British were still sending sabotage instructions and orders to assassinate Dutch collaborators, and were still eager for information and intelligence reports. Giskes had been wrong in thinking that they would suddenly break off the game. Instead, they were letting the idyll die a natural death.

By Christmas 1943, Giskes – whose office had been transferred to Driebergen – was still wondering whether London had discovered the truth at last. And if so, had they discovered the whole truth? Their tone had changed. It was as if the radio operators had been replaced by a robot. The warmth of humanity had gone from the messages, there was no friendly word interspersed here and there. They no longer ended with 'Good Luck'. They had become fabricated and meaningless.

Giskes came to the conclusion that the British were maintaining contact with the sole aim of saving the lives of the captured agents. He became quite convinced that London had finally understood when, on 5 January 1944, they informed him that future parachute drops for the Dutch Resistance would be directed to Belgium. This time there was no possible doubt. The 'English Game' was over!

It had lasted twenty-one months and twelve days, beating the record for a *Funkspiel* by more than sixteen months. This feat was never to be surpassed, not even in the postwar years.

Giskes was left with the problem of ridding himself of the radio links with London. He was like some giant spider caught up in its own web. He could simply stop transmitting altogether and transfer the radio operators and cipher clerks engaged in the *England Spiel* to other duties. (When the *Abwehr* was taken over by the SS, Giskes had converted his 111/F Section into a 'Field Espionage Section', to avoid coming under Himmler's orders.) But Giskes wanted to bow himself out, to end on a note of sarcasm which would do him honour. He composed a final message for London, which he sent on 4 March 1944.

'To Messrs Blunt, Bingham and Successors Ltd stop you are trying to do business in the Netherlands without our assistance stop we think this rather unfair in view our long and successful cooperation as your sole agent stop but never mind whenever you decide to come and pay a visit to the continent you may be assured that you will be received with same care and result as all those you sent us before stop hoping to see you soon message ends.'

Nevertheless, his heart was very heavy. A fine operation, the best of all those mounted by the *Abewhr*, and to end like that! The results of it were plain for all to see, there in Haaren prison – fifty-six agents, many of whom had eventually cooperated with the Germans.

After twenty-one months of secret warfare in which the Germans had triumphed hands down, an end had had to be put to it! For in Giskes's mind there were no doubts – the British had been duped from beginning to end. (It must be remembered that he was still unaware that Lauwers had tricked him from the start, over the security check, and that he did not know Jordaan had sent out an SOS, that Dourlein and others had smuggled messages out of prison.) Giskes did not believe that 'Plan Holland' had been a ruse, an attempt to distract the attention of the German High Command at the time of the Dieppe raid. He had clamped down on British espionage and subversive activities in Holland, and that was all he cared to know. After the war, the matter would be investigated. But for the moment he had other things on his mind. He had to make a good show, to save his honour as a soldier among the ruins of the Third Reich.

There were the captured agents – Giskes had promised that their lives would be spared. It was not the kind of promise easy to keep!

After March 1944, it had become impossible to make Rauter believe that the SOE agents were still of use for anything. So they were going to die.

However, the SIPO, the SD and the rest of the Himmler machine were in such a frenzy of repressive measures (attacks on German soldiers were increasing) that there was no question of putting the agents on trial. But neither was anyone in authority prepared to order their summary execution. Not even the most bloodthirsty of the SS, in 1944, wanted to have to account later to the Allies for another massacre of prisoners. So the SOE agents were to be quietly 'liquidated'. They would quietly disappear into the shadows. They were out of Giskes's control, but he did all in his power to try to save them. In April, he managed to have

Lauwers and Jordaan kept at Haaren when the others were transferred.

Lauwers had no wish for this distinction which marked him out as *the* traitor. Giskes visited him in his cell on 14 April – the first time the two had been face to face since the previous autumn. Giskes was in civilian clothes, as usual when he wanted to convince or win over someone. He offered a cigarette to Lauwers, a Lauwers who was weak and thin, who hardly slept at night and who was still wondering if he had been betrayed, and by whom.

'I'm trying to protect you right to the end,' Giskes began. 'You've been most useful to me. There would have been no *England Spiel* without you.'

Lauwers jumped up at that. He could hardly speak for rage. He was literally foaming at the mouth.

'I've never helped you!' he cried. 'I did all I could to spoil it! For six months, I sent a false security check – and that's not all. I sent several messages to warn the British! I tricked you all the way through, right from the start. And the British understood, I'm sure of that. They just pretended not to. You're the one who lost!'

It was obvious that Giskes thought the other's mind was going. He tried to calm him.

'It's possible, Lauwers, quite possible. But in heaven's name, my friend, if you're put on trial don't say all that to the judges!'

Lauwers gave a shrug. 'I'm no friend of yours. You're going to have all my comrades killed, and you want me to be saved. I won't have it!'

Giskes did not pursue the matter. He left the cell. But he arranged matters so that neither Lauwers nor Jordaan was sent to Germany with the other agents.

At the end of July 1944, the other SOE agents were removed from Assen prison, where they had been transferred earlier from Haaren, and were taken in three lorries to the camp at Vught, near Hertogenbosch. They had not yet entered the awful realm of concentration and extermination camps. Vught was a transit camp. None of them, according to witnesses, appeared to rebel against his fate. They had all been expecting it for a long time. But they knew nothing about extermination camps, and were just thankful to have escaped the firing squad. But

Jambroes, apparently, said to one of the SS guards, 'You might just as well have shot us straight away.' To which the German replied: 'You've lost nothing by waiting.' Baatsen, it is reported, was still singing. Lauwers and Jordaan were not in the convoy. The agents were still wearing the clothes they had landed in, the famous double-breasted, ready-made suits which were their uniform. But not for much longer.

On 24 August, at five in the morning, they were suddenly and brutally packed into cattle-trucks with five hundred political prisoners. (Until this moment the agents had been treated neither better nor worse than prisoners anywhere in the world.) The doors were slid shut and locked on them. And they realised that death was not far off. Some of them became panic-stricken, alternately imploring and shouting their hatred, cursing the British who had sent them to this, the Germans who were going to kill them, and Lauwers who had betrayed them. Crammed together in the cattle-trucks, the journey lasted two days and nights.

Early on the third day, the train jolted to a final halt and the doors were slid open. The living and the dead were pulled out. They were at the entrance to Mauthausen concentration camp. By some macabre miracle, not a single SOE agent had died during the terrible journey.

They were all put in the same barrack hut. Some still thought that they would receive favourable treatment in this hell on earth, but they were quickly disillusioned. Their civilian clothes were taken from them and they were given the striped garments of concentration camp inmates. Then they were marched off to a quarry and put to work, being made to carry large blocks of stone. There were bursts of firing all day long. The quarry also served as an execution ground, and at Mauthausen there were executions from dawn to dusk.

On 6 September 1944, twenty Dutch agents were taken out of the work-gang, but had to go to the quarry all the same. They realised what this meant. The SS officer in charge of the firing squad (he was barely twenty years of age) told them to line up at a stone wall with their backs to their killers. No sentence was read out, they were not told why they were being shot—it was as though their execution was in the natural order of things.

The following morning another twenty agents were shot in the same manner. By the evening of 7 September there were less than a dozen of them left, and they knew they would be dead in the morning. It was then that an amazing incident occurred – the first and last act of open revolt by any of the agents. One of them (he has never been identified) asked to see the camp commandant, saying that it was important and that one could not refuse the request of a man who was to be shot next morning. The camp commandant agreed to see him. This Dutch agent was taken to the commandant's office by an armed SS. He clicked his heels in salute and presented his case quietly and deliberately.

'Commandant, I wish to bring to your notice that a grave injustice has been committed with regard to my Dutch comrades and myself. We are treated like spies. We are given quarters with common criminals. But we are soldiers. Personally, I hold the rank of lieutenant and I am a Knight Cross of the Order of William of Orange, fourth class. I demand to be treated as a soldier, by soldiers, even though they are Germans.'

The SS commandant let him finish, showing no sign of annoyance or wrath. He had the face of a bureaucrat, not unlike Himmler's.

'I understand,' he said. 'Thank you for bringing this very interesting matter to my notice. You are quite right, you and the others are not spies. But tell me – when you were captured, I take it that you were in uniform?'

'No, Commandant. I was in civilian clothes. My mission required it.'

'Quite so. Tomorrow morning, you and your comrades will be shot because,' (he sprang from his chair, shouting) 'we shoot all guerilla fighters! It's a rule of war, mister lieutenant!'

And at dawn on 8 September 1944, the remaining SOE agents were executed.

PART FOUR *The Summing Up*

The Summing Up

Schreieder is still alive. So is Giskes. These two elusive customers avoided capture until the end of the war. But Giskes must have played his cards very cleverly to have escaped arrest, and worse, by the Himmlerites. Canaris was hanged by the SS on 9 April 1945, at Flossenburg prison. His friends and disciples, Giskes among them, were openly accused of intelligence with the enemy. Fortunately for him, he had many friends in Berlin and they supported his claim that the *England Spiel* had been of immense benefit to the Third Reich. Nevertheless, he was a man under reprieve when the British arrested him in May 1945.

Today, Giskes lives quietly at Starnberg, near Munich. I went to see him, and found a tall, straight-backed old man who pays great attention to his health and physical condition. At seventy years of age he still goes horse-riding and frequently has a swim in the icy lake. His eyes sparkle when he talks about his *Abwehr* career. On his mantelpiece, between some African spears and a small bronze bust, stands a souvenir of Operation North Pole – a metal flask with Giskes's initials on it. A similar flask was presented to each of the Germans who had taken part in the operation. The flasks had belonged to the SOE agents parachuted into Holland.

'From beginning to end, that's to say until my final message, the British were taken in,' Giskes maintained. 'The proof is in the fact that we received some very important information from them, for instance the dates of bombing raids and their objectives. This information was always correct. And information sent to radio posts controlled by us enabled our fighter planes and ack-ack to break up many Allied air attacks. Lauwers's messages? Yes, but I'd like to see them first. Lauwers is an officer for whom I've great respect, and he's very loyal – he admitted to me, at the end, that he had continued warning the British. But imagine his position after the war – discredited, almost a war criminal. It was only natural that he should make up this story of sending warning messages and giving a false security check, in order to clear himself.'

More than twenty years afterwards, Giskes, with an air of the utmost kindness, was still trying to poison poor Lauwers's life. Lauwers really had turned traitor; he could not have done anything else. He had turned traitor to try to save the lives of those parachuted after him. Such was still the view of retired *Abwehr* officer Hermann Giskes.

It is understandable that he should wish to prevent an unfortunate 'turned' agent from robbing him of his glory. But there is more to it than that. In effect, the British had reacted on the whole as if they were duped throughout by the *Abwehr*.

In the first place (and this is Giskes's second line of argument), if the British had wanted to deceive the Germans in their turn, there was no need to despatch fifty agents – fifty! – to fall into the Gestapo's clutches. One radio link would have been sufficient.

Secondly (Giskes's third point), apart from a few doubtful missions, such as the Kootwijk raid, the sabotage action ordered to be carried out as part of 'Plan Holland' was all against important objectives – warships in Rotterdam harbour, rail communications, Luftwaffe installations, and so on.

'Besides,' said Giskes, 'the British never knew that the Dutch Resistance had been completely broken up. Even after the arrest of Vorrink and D'Aquin, even after the final break between London and the *Abwehr*, the British still believed there were a number of SOE agents organising and training a large secret army. The proof is in the fact that when Montgomery launched the Arnhem operation he was counting on his airborne forces receiving support from local Resistance groups. The absence of them hastened the disaster. Montgomery himself wrote as much. In September 1944, neither Baker Street nor the War Office realised just how great was the collapse of SOE plans in Holland!

'And all that was due to the amateurish way in which the British had gone about organising SOE,' Giskes concluded. 'They built it up too hastily and set in motion a machinery which was too vast, too ambitious, for the means at their disposal. SOE needed professional Intelligence officers at its head, as we had in the *Abwehr*, and in particular it needed men who were adept at subversive warfare. Instead, they sent us infants, keen and willing but quite unfitted for that kind of combat. It was the same thing at Baker Street. Because SOE was concerned with sabotage and not with Intelligence work, there were only two experts in espionage on the headquarters staff, Colonel Cordeaux and Mr Seymour. Two out of nine! I'm quite sure that the radio messages were deciphered by army clerks without any experience and who did it automatically, never bringing a critical mind to bear on their work. I repeat, it's not at all surprising that the British believed in our fables for so long.'

Joseph Schreieder now lives in Munich. He has only recently retired (in 1966), being younger than Giskes. I would even say that until then the *Kriminalrat* had more work than he could cope with. I met him in the bar of the Eden Wolf Hotel in Munich – a plump little man easily recognisable from the descriptions given to me here and there. He had hardly aged at all, to judge from a photograph taken in 1945. He was accompanied by a giant of a man clad in a leather coat, whom he introduced as his chief assistant.

I had been dreading the moment when, for the first time in my life, I should have to shake hands with a Gestapo officer. Well, it was soon done, I had pressed the little hand held out to me. It was soft and slim, still with dirty finger-nails, a hand made for drawing rather than strangling. Schreieder ordered tea, as it was late afternoon. Then he began by doing his little act. He drew a card from an inside pocket and read from it.

'You are Philippe Ganier-Raymond, born in ——— on ... The son of ... and ... Went to school at the Lycée Janson de Sailly and then at Louis-le-Grand, in Paris. You've been a journalist since August 1957. *Und so weiter . . .*' He read out my life history with amazing accuracy – the date of my marriage, the names of my children. There were scraps of intimate details on his card such as one never tells one's best friends. I could have killed him!

I could have killed the police officer in Paris too, or whoever it was who had given my pedigree to this ex-Nazi copper over the telephone, just like that. For I had made my appointment with the *Kriminalrat* only twenty-four hours beforehand, so there had been no time for him to make proper enquiries. However.

173

Then I suddenly understood it all! Joseph's little act was worth more than all the descriptions of the brain-washing of the SOE agents. For a few minutes I had been Dourlein – or Baatsen or Kloos – in other words, someone who was expected and about whom everything was known, and to whom one roundly explained that it was all child's play and that the Intelligence services had the tabs on you right from the start. I could understand their anger – Dourlein's anger, Kloos's anger – on feeling my own. If I was angry with the French official who had so generously provided a German colleague with information, how much greater must have been the agents' rage against the British. You could never have made them believe that they had not been betrayed from the moment they left England! How admirable, then, was the conduct of Lauwers, who had stood up to Giskes and debated the situation with him. Schreieder admitted to me: 'That's the method I used with the agents in the "English Game".' I calmed down. I even smiled when he leaned towards me and confided a State secret known to at least three-quarters of the population of Munich. 'I'm doing similar work now – against the Communists. So don't mention my name.'

The little man was well organised and youthful. Giskes could not have found a better collaborator for his *England Spiel*. The fact remained that I could not be sure of anything he said. Schreieder lies a lot, and is not very good at it either. For instance, he told me that from 1942 onwards he and his department had all the *Abwehr* services in Holland under their control, that Van der Waals was pure at heart, that Giskes was 'an unruly subordinate who had to be put in his place on several occasions', and that he, Schreieder, had never had anyone tortured, neither before nor during the *England Spiel*. (Tell that to the surviving Sudeten Jews and Dutch Jews!)

I put three questions to him about the *England Spiel*.

1. *At what date did he think the British began to suspect the truth?* 'September 1942. At the very latest, November.'

2. *So they afterwards despatched seventeen agents knowing full well what the situation was?* 'Not necessarily. They certainly knew, and had known for several months, that there was something wrong. There can be no doubt that Jongelie and Macare were dropped on 25 October with orders to check on the radio

posts. But the British were not sure of anything. It wasn't until my dear comrade Giskes crossed the T's for them that they understood what had happened. And even then, it was only at the end of the war that they fully realised the extent of the disaster.'

3. *How had he ended the war?* 'As a soldier. And you can take it from me that I had become rather popular with the Dutch. Oh yes. Listen – I'll tell you what happened at the end of my time in Holland. . . .'

And an amazing story it was, as Schreieder told it. The Allies had liberated Brabant by September 1944, but most of Holland was still occupied by the Germans and the population suffered from famine throughout that winter. In March 1945, a certain 'Council of Trustworthy Men' consisting of representatives of right-wing Resistance groups, leading citizens of The Hague and several clergy, decided to play the part of the Burgesses of Calais with the Nazi authorities. There could be no question of negotiating the salvation of the Dutch people with that madman, Rauter, and so the deputation approached Schreieder, whose reputation as a humane policeman had spread even to the Resistance. An appointment was made by telephone.

On 9 March 1945, at ten in the morning, an old car stopped in front of the Binnenhoff and four elderly men, including a pastor, got out. Schreieder was waiting for them at the top of the steps. He ushered the four very embarrassed men into his office. The meeting lasted two hours. At first, the Dutch deputation was very wary, but Schreieder's openness cleared the atmosphere and an agreement was reached. The terms of it were that the Resistance groups agreed to cease their attacks on German troops, and in return the Germans would freely allow the population to collect the food supplies which the Allies were dropping by parachute. Eventually German troops would distribute the food.

But every agreement, especially a verbal one, requires guarantees. Although Schreieder did not say so, it is highly probable that he and the 'Trustworthy Men' came to an exchange arrangement. The *Kriminalrat* delivered up a few V-men to the rough justice of the Resistance, and in exchange was given the names and hideouts of some Communist partisans. In this way, neither side lost face. At least, such is the story often told at The Hague.

The four men left Schreieder's office at midday, greatly relieved. It had begun to snow, and they hurried to their car. But, alas, the engine refused to start. The pastor, who was at the wheel, kept pulling out the self-starter, but a loud growl was the only result. A small crowd began to form. By now, a score of people suspected that these well-known citizens had been making some arrangement with the Gestapo.

The pastor, red in the face, got out holding a starting handle and began winding furiously. But all to no avail. It was then that Schreieder, who had been watching from the main doorway, called to one of his men; and a couple of minutes later a black Mercedes (the largest one, for high-ranking officials) drew up right behind the pastor's old car.

'Can I help you, gentlemen?' asked the German driver. The situation being what it was, the pastor got in, the Mercedes began to push his car, the engine finally started up – and Schreieder called after them in Dutch, cupping his hands to his mouth so that at least fifty people could hear: 'Lucky there's still the Gestapo to get your Resistance going!'

And Joseph Schreieder's activities in Holland ended on that derisive note.

He was later arrested by the Allies in the Rhineland, as a potential war criminal. He attended many interrogation sessions, but was eventually released in 1948 and resumed his police career in Bavaria.

Incidentally, Harster, Schreieder's immediate superior at The Hague from 1941 to 1944, was arrested in Munich in January 1966, following the remorse with which the German Federal Republic had been overcome.

As for those prominent V-men, Ridderhoff and Van der Waals, the former was sentenced to death in 1946. However, there is no record in Dutch judicial records of his execution nor of his being pardoned. Dourlein told me that he was living under an assumed name in a suburb of The Hague.

The postwar story of Van der Waals is even odder. The Dutch Resistance was naturally after his blood, but he had wisely disappeared. His whereabouts were eventually discovered by a Dutch colonel on a diplomatic mission in Berlin. For eight months, Antonius had been working in the Russian Zone as a British agent. As indefatigable as ever, his mission was to uncover the agents whom the Russians were introducing into the convoys of POWs and deportees being returned to the West. The British said that they were satisfied with his services. They were so satisfied that they hesitated a long time before handing over to the Dutch 'this agent who has done useful work for us "for several years".' When the Dutch finally had Van der Waals in their custody, they soon brought him to trial (Schreieder was one of the witnesses) and he was sentenced to death.

Right until the morning of his execution, Antonius maintained that he was a British agent who had been working inside the Gestapo. But the British did nothing to save him, and for good reason. His claim can hardly be taken seriously, especially when it is the last resort of a man under sentence of death. And yet, what had caused the British to hesitate so long before handing him over to the Dutch? One can only surmise. Moreover, Van der Waals remained perfectly calm right until the end (all those concerned are agreed on this point). This is most surprising when one remembers his behaviour when scared for his own safety. He probably thought someone would intervene to prevent his sentence being carried out. Who or what could have given Antonius this wild hope? It is only one of the many mysteries in this long affair.

There is an even stranger one. On the night of 14 February 1943, when the *England Spiel* was almost a year old, Schreieder and some of his men were out in the wind and rain waiting to receive the tenth drop of agents and containers. Punctually at midnight, a Halifax appeared through the clouds; it circled the dropping zone twice, then a human figure descended. The landing was a rough one – a gust of wind drove the parachute across the field. Schreieder's men hurried to the spot and found the agent lying inert on the ground. Dead, or just suffering from concussion? A V-man took the helmet off – and long dark hair stained with blood uncoiled to shoulder length.

'A woman!'

When Beatrix Terwindt, a former stewardess of the KLM airline, regained consciousness she found herself in bed in a white-walled room. A coarse, grey army blanket was tickling the palms of her hands. She gradually became aware of a dull throbbing in her head. She put a hand to her hair in an instinctive feminine gesture, and her fingers met a thick, tight bandage. A nurse was standing with her back turned, and Beatrix could hear some water bubbling. She asked in English for a cup of tea with sugar, and the nurse spun round. There was a swastika sewn above the pocket of her blouse. She spoke sternly to Beatrix in German, telling her to be quiet and wait. Beatrix saw a bunch of keys dangling from her belt.

It all came back to her – she remembered the months of training in England, a training which had shattered the nerves of a good many men. She had successfully passed all the stages, obtaining high marks in rapid firing. And then one fine day she had been taken to an aerodrome in the south-east and put in a barrack hut by herself. She remembered the morning when Captain Lieftinck had come in to tell her about her mission. She was being sent to organise escape routes for some Dutch Resistance groups. A list of addresses would be given to her just before departure. Then Lieftinck had left as abruptly as he had entered.

At this point in her recollections, Schreieder appeared in the room. Nothing is so startling as seeing a green-and-black army uniform in a hospital ward, even in a military hospital. Schreieder had his cap in his hand and seemed ill at ease. 'Good morning,' he said. 'I've just seen the doctor, and he tells me that your injuries are superficial. You'll be allowed to get up tomorrow. I'm glad of that. We shall be able to have a talk.' Beatrix replied that she had nothing to tell him. Schreieder left.

After Lieftinck had been to see her, several days passed without incident. She saw Captain Neave several times; he always seemed very busy, hurrying about with a number of files under his arm. He was apparently in charge of the despatch of agents. She liked Neave's frank ways and high spirits. Once or twice they met in the evening in the officers' bar.

Beatrix had often wondered whether the work for which she had volunteered would be beyond her strength and capacities. Neave reassured her. 'The best Intelligence agents have always been women – history shows that.' Nevertheless, she felt that her five feet two inches and one hundred and ten pounds put her at a disadvantage.

When Schreieder had left, the grey mouse of a nurse brought her a cup of tea. 'Drink it while it's hot,' she said, more of a nurse than a jailer for a moment. Beatrix gulped it down and put the cup on the side table. 'My head's bad,' she complained, gently touching her hair. The nurse disappeared, to return ten minutes later carrying a saucepan of boiling water with a syringe in it. 'I'll give you an injection,' she said, 'and you'll sleep for twelve hours.' Beatrix held out her arm . . . and slept the clock round.

She could remember little else of what had happened up to the time of jumping from the plane. When she woke after her long sleep, the injection seemed to have eliminated all recent events from her mind. She must have got into the plane, she told herself. She could still hear the engines revving up. And she must have said goodbye to a few people, but whom? Then she had jumped. Had she been scared? There could be no doubt of that. During her parachute training she had thought she was jumping to her death each time she dropped from the captive balloon. But she could not remember anything of those last few minutes in England!

When Schreieder came to fetch her, she was up and dressed in a nurse's uniform. With the bandage round her head and with her pale cheeks she looked like a religious novice. Two male nurses helped her out to the car – an old Mercedes that was still painted with the brownish-yellow camouflage of the Afrika Korps. Schreieder said not a word to her during the journey. He was waiting to be seated behind his office desk at the Binnenhoff before questioning her. He then showed every consideration for her condition. 'Take your time, I'm sure you are going to reply.'

He began by asking her 'the names of the irresponsible cowards who had dared to send a woman to carry out shameful acts of sabotage that they were afraid of doing themselves'. Beatrix burst out laughing, then grimaced with pain as she felt the drag on the stitches in her head-wound. Schreieder thought she was going to faint, and rose from his chair, but she gestured that she was all right and he could continue.

He put more questions, but she did not reply. Her thoughts were elsewhere. The events just before her departure from England were coming back to her in flashes. The plump, sweating German officer opposite her was of no significance whatever. Only one question was on her mind – how did she come to be here? There was no doubt that they had been expecting her. Besides, the German said just then, as though establishing a link between them : 'All the other agents have been captured, you know. You're the thirty-ninth. But the first woman. They must be getting shorthanded in England.'

Schreieder made a mistake in trying to be witty. Beatrix started up and, forgetting the stitches in her head, cried out: 'I'm not telling you a thing! You won't learn anything from me!'

She was taken to the women's prison and put in a cell with a woman who was probably a stool-pigeon. The effects of the injection had worn off. The memories of her last days in England were coming back more and more clearly, but it all seemed to have happened to somebody else, who had told her about it.

She saw an officer in her mind's eye ... the evening of her departure, at about nine o'clock. Yes, and Lieftinck was with him. The three of them had had a drink in the mess, then driven out to the aircraft waiting on the runway. Lieftinck had handed her a flask. She had unscrewed the cap and smelt the contents – Dutch gin. And then what? There had been a few words spoken. Someone had said – what had he said?

Beatrix slept the clock round again on her prison bed, and would probably have slept even longer if a nurse had not entered the cell to change the dressing on her head wound. An hour later, she was in Schreieder's office again and being asked the same questions – what was her mission, what were the names of her chiefs, the addresses of the people she had been told to contact? Schreieder was not very insistent. Beatrix realised, despite her headache, that he already knew the answers. She refused to say anything. Somehow she knew that no harm would come to her.

She could feel the pain in her head now, but her brain was clearer. And while telling Schreieder that he would learn nothing from her, she was gradually filling the blanks in her memory, like the squares in a crossword puzzle. They were all complete now – except one. Except for a few words that someone had said to her.

They came back to her while in the car returning her to the prison. It was at the foot of the aircraft. She had been about to climb the tubular ladder when she felt a hand on her shoulder. She had turned and seen a British officer. He had grasped her right hand and said with a little smile: 'Be careful, Miss Terwindt. *Don't be caught like the others.*'

Beatrix Terwindt was interrogated several times by the Gestapo but never told them anything. Schreieder kept her in prison in Holland until the big convoy to Mauthausen in July 1944. But she was sent to Ravensbruck, and was still alive when the British liberated the camp in May 1945.

In Holland, she is a national heroine. She was married ten years ago, and now lives in Utrecht. I met her there. She is still a beautiful woman beneath a face marked by suffering. She told me that she would never be quite a normal woman again.

Don't be caught like the others![1]

These words constitute the first entry in the file on the *England Spiel*. They prove that at least one British officer *knew*.

What had happened to Ubbink and Dourlein – those two fanatics for liberty who may have upset the 'English Game'? When they at last stopped running through the back streets of Haaren they both thought that the worst was over. They thought it would be child's play to cross Europe, in comparison with the well-nigh impossible escape they had just accomplished. Nevertheless, they controlled their high spirits. The first and urgent need was to find a safe shelter, then an escape line.

They walked to Tilburg, the nearest town, and there the priest of the Catholic church took them in, though rather unwillingly. The following day, a police officer, Van Bilsen, who 'worked for the Resistance' and to whom the priest had sent word, entered the shed where they were hiding. They told him their story, but he obviously did not believe it. He went away saying that he would get in touch with London and find out whether the agents Dourlein and Ubbink were known. An hour later he was back, all smiles. He showed them a poster.

'Read this.'

It was one of Schreieder's notices. The town was plastered with them.

---

[1] This phrase, 'don't be caught like the others', was not revealed by Trix Terwindt until much later to close friends. When I met her, in November 1965, she repeated it to me, adding that she did not accept at all that the English were culpable in the North Pole affair.

REWARD 500 GUILDERS

WANTED

For Burglary and House-Breaking
Johan Bernhard Ubbink,
former officer in the Merchant Navy
and
Pieter Dourlein, bricklayer.

Their photos were on the poster, two bad reproductions of police photos. They were unrecognisable. Van Bilsen told them that the town was swarming with police and tracker dogs. Such an intensive search would not be made for two miserable burglars. 'I believe you now,' he said. And he hid them for two months.

In the meantime, Dourlein sent an indignant letter to the Gestapo at The Hague, informing Messrs Schreieder and company that (a) he had never been a bricklayer, and held the rank of Petty Officer in the Dutch Navy, (b) he had never committed a burglary, (c) a reward of five hundred guilders for two patriots such as Ubbink and himself was really not enough. 'The two of us are worth at least five thousand guilders,' he wrote, and ended his letter: 'But it is of no importance, as in any case you will never catch us.'[1]

On 11 November 1943 (the search for them having been called off a fortnight previously) they boarded a train for Antwerp dressed as workmen. They had been supplied with false identity papers which were miniature works of art (if only SOE had had such good forgers!). Three days later they were in Paris, having travelled via Brussels and Mons. Van Bilsen had given them an address to go to, but they had some difficulty in finding it. Neither of them had been in Paris before. The address turned out to be that of another priest. Van Bilsen was obviously a man of earnest character.

The priest put them on an escape route to Switzerland – apparently the one to Spain was too risky at the time. They successfully crossed the frontier (how many of those who helped them on their way were Christmann's men?) and they reached Berne towards the end of November. They made straight for the British Legation and asked to see the officer in charge of Intelligence

[1] Dourlein, P., *Inside North Pole* (Kimber, London, 1953).

matters. In the large waiting-room with plush curtains they saw their faces in a mirror, and they hardly recognised the sallow, dirty, thin features of the two scarecrows that stared back at them. The Intelligence officer came in. He could not have been more than twenty-five, was wearing a club tie and spoke with a cultured accent. He hesitated at the sight of the two tramps, then took them to his office. Ubbink and Dourlein, relaying one another, told him their story – the drop into Holland, their capture by the Gestapo, Schreieder, prison, the escape, Van Bilsen, their journey from Holland. The young man listened in amazement. When they had finished, he cupped his chin in his hands and said, 'Fascinating.'

He repeated it, seemed to be searching for other words but could not find any. Then he got up and went into the adjoining office. A quarter of an hour passed before he returned, but he had his words all ready.

'Well now, what you've done is quite amazing. We greatly admire your courage. We shall inform London this evening, but in the meantime you must be in need of a good rest. I've arranged for a car to come and take you to a good hotel.' Dourlein and Ubbink were too tired to realise that they were being got rid of rather than looked after. All they could think of was that they would soon be able to sleep in peace and comfort.

The following day, the Dutch military attaché, Major-General Van Tricht, called to see them at the hotel. This time, they were warmly greeted and congratulated. They certainly needed it. The previous day, at the British Legation, they had had the impression of being something of a nuisance, of upsetting the apple-cart. But that may well have been due to their tiredness and, besides, they had been on edge. Van Tricht, however, was most effusive, full of praise, telling them that he had known of their escape through messages from the Dutch Resistance. There was just one thing. He hesitated, then said: 'Now you have to prove to *them* that you really are Ubbink and Dourlein.'

This was not easy; they had no identity papers in their real names. But there would be no difficulty once they reached England, and it was important for them to go there.

'I'll try to arrange it,' said Van Tricht. 'In the meantime, rest and get your strength back. You've got five days. Then the Swiss will feel obliged to intern you, but between then and now –'

He left them and went straight to the British Legation, where he was assured that the case of Ubbink and Dourlein was now quite clear. They were fine fellows, heroes in fact, and should be helped to reach England as soon as possible. Information had been received about them.

On 28 November, Ubbink and Dourlein crossed the frontier into France again, having been given clean clothes and money. By way of Lyons, Marseilles and Cerbère, they reached the Spanish frontier, travelling by train (they deliberately chose compartments full of German soldiers, as there was never any snap identity check). On the evening of 1 December they were in Spain, and spent the night at a farmhouse. Several days later, they reached Madrid and made their way to the Dutch Embassy.

The military attaché was absent, and they were received by a woman official who was in her forties, tall, wore no make-up, and with her hair drawn tightly back in a bun had the appearance of a pastor's wife. Her attitude was reserved. When they had finished telling their story, she gave Ubbink pen and paper and told him to write out a full report. 'Don't leave out any details,' she warned.

They did as they were bidden. They were not expecting to be decorated, but a few friendly words would not have come amiss – and would have cost the official nothing. Instead, she treated them with the chilly suspicion of officials who dislike having their routine disturbed by 'special cases'. Ubbink and Dourlein had brought the sounds and stinks of war into this haven of neutrality. It was also probable that she did not believe a word of their story. They finished their written report, and were then told that a room had been reserved for them at the Velasquez Hotel and they would be seen by officials from the British Embassy.

The two were baffled by it all. They could not understand why the woman should seem so eager to have as little as possible to do with them. There were no questions in their minds. They were just slightly indignant at receiving such treatment from a compatriot.

They spent many days kicking their heels in Madrid. They were summoned to the British Embassy several times, and had to tell their story all over again. They were given forms to fill in. Dourlein clenched his fists. While they were wandering about

Madrid, where signs of the civil war were still in evidence, the SOE agents in prison were in danger of being shot and perhaps others were still being dropped into Holland. At the British Embassy he had been told that the necessary steps had been taken and that the 'game' had come to an end. But it had been said so feebly, with such little interest, that he and Ubbink were becoming anxious. Had the Embassy official really done what he said? Were they being taken for a couple of swindlers or imposters, maniacs or spies? However, it would all be cleared up in London. They had been promised that they would be flown there 'as soon as circumstances permitted'.

In the meantime, they became irritated by the attitude of indifference tinged with suspicion which the British and Dutch officials adopted towards them. It was as in Berne – the diplomats of belligerent countries did their utmost to keep aloof from this war, having been fortunately spared it. Ubbink and Dourlein were also wondering with some bitterness why London delayed their return, knowing who they were and what they had done.

At last, on 30 January 1944, a British Embassy car took them to Gibraltar. Two days later they were put aboard a RAF plane. In a few hours they would be back in England, back from their mission. Now they were happy. The plane landed at an airfield near Bristol. It was raining. The propellers had hardly stopped spinning when a RAF police sergeant appeared at the door, dripping wet.

'Ubbink? Dourlein? You two? Come with me, please.'

He tried to be more welcoming in the truck taking them across the airfield to the office buildings. 'I must congratulate you,' he said. 'Very few come back from their missions these days.'

But that could mean anything. Two men were waiting for them in the briefing room, and there was no mistaking their profession – with their felt hats and raincoats, they might have stepped straight from a detective film. One of them showed his card, the other said, 'Come with us, please.'

But this was impossible – surely they weren't being arrested! 'We want to see Colonel De Bruyne straight away!' cried Dourlein. 'Straight away, d'you hear?'

'I'm sorry, but that's not possible just now,' said the one who had shown his card.

They each took one of the Dutchmen by his arm, with just a

little less firmness than had Schreieder's men when he was captured after landing. Their astonishment was greater than their anger, and neither made any further protest. They had been expected for some time, to judge by the bungalow which was ready for them at Guildford, just outside London. Their beds were made and there were some Dutch books on the shelves. Two counter-intelligence officers came to question them every morning, and they told their story yet again. Dourlein kept clamouring that he wanted to see Lieftinck or De Bruyne, to which the British officers quietly replied that it was not possible for the moment. Ubbink did his best to calm Dourlein, knowing that he was capable of strangling one of the officers in his wrath.

Their interrogation lasted for several weeks. They wrote to both Lieftinck and De Bruyne, who eventually replied that the matter would be cleared up one day, and that in the meantime they must not lose their heads.

During one interrogation session, Ubbink mentioned the Tilburg police officer, Van Bilsen. The following morning, the Intelligence officers returned to this point.

'You did say Van Bilsen, the police officer?' asked one. 'That's odd.' He gave a twisted smile. 'Van Bilsen was a Gestapo agent. Moreover, he was shot a month ago by some of the Limburg Resistance. Your story is not very clear.'

'Not at all clear,' added his colleague.

So murky did it seem that the following day the two Dutchmen found themselves in Brixton Prison! They still thought some mistake had been made, the most glaring mistake of the war! They continued sending letters (they had been put in the same cell) to their chiefs at the SOE Dutch Section, De Bruyne and Lieftinck, who were their last hope. And early in May the two arrived at Brixton to see Dourlein and Ubbink.

'Keep up your courage,' said Lieftinck. 'You'll be out of here before long. We believe in you, of course. But unfortunately the British have their doubts about you. They received a mysterious message from Holland saying that you were working for the Germans (the message sent by Giskes?), and they are not yet convinced of the contrary. In any case, you can take it for certain that no more agents are being parachuted into Holland.'

A week later the two officers were back to tell Ubbink and Dourlein that they were being released. How embarrassed and sheepish the two officers were! In the meantime, a V1 had fallen on the prison and Dourlein was injured rather badly about the head. Hurt in body, embittered and depressed, this courageous man who had been so humiliated became intent on seeking death in battle. As soon as he recovered from his head injury he joined the Dutch Air Force and was trained as a gunner. He took part in the final battles for Holland's liberation with RAF 320 Squadron. He had not found death, but he had aged a great deal.

I went to see Pieter Dourlein in 1964. He was still in the Navy, and working at the Admiralty in The Hague. He was a great help to me in my researches for this book. In 1963 he had learned that the message he smuggled out of Haaren Prison had reached London via Berne, quite readable. What was he to think? He does not know, he does not want to know. He is a married man now, his wife is English, and they have a son. He will soon be retiring from the service. 'Then I'd like to work as a commercial traveller for some big firm, Philips for instance,' he told me. 'I'd very much like to travel.' The fact is, he would rather not know the real truth behind his experiences.

'The British played their tricks on me, I know. But I shouldn't like to have it proved. I was rehabilitated after the war, and was even awarded a medal ten years later. But that doesn't wipe anything out. That doesn't help me forget that forty-eight of my comrades lost their lives, and it will never be known why.'

There are several questions that Pieter Dourlein still cannot help going over:

1. Why was no notice taken of his message from Haaren Prison which reached London at the beginning of August 1943?

2. When Dourlein was parachuted into Holland, did the British know that all the SOE agents despatched to Holland had been captured and that some had been turned?

3. Why was there so much negligence? – badly forged identity papers, money that had been withdrawn from circulation, English labels left on clothing?

4. What reason had the British for isolating and then imprisoning Ubbink and Dourlein when they returned to England? The British knew quite well that neither of them was a Gestapo agent. (An Intelligence report to this effect had reached the War Office while the two were still in Spain.) Besides, Operation North Pole

had come to an end some time previously. Several Resistance groups had sent messages verifying that Ubbink and Dourlein were heroes without blemish. And in May 1944 everyone concerned knew that the message denouncing them had been sent by Giskes.

'We were a nuisance, the cumbersome witnesses of some dirty work,' concludes Dourlein. 'We had to be kept away from other Dutchmen in England. This is all that Dourlein has to say. Ubbink is still alive too, but he has nothing to say. He is in the Dutch diplomatic service, in South Africa, and is bound by the official secrets' act.

After the war, furious voices were raised in Holland demanding that the truth be told about the *whole* of the operation. Fortyeight of their compatriots had been murdered, and no one knew why. But the Dutch nation was still weak and starved, dependent upon her powerful allies. To ask for justice, perhaps to accuse Britain, was beyond her strength just then.

Nevertheless, there was one man determined to establish the truth. His name was Doctor L. A. Donker, an upright and just magistrate if ever there was one. In 1947, at the request of the Dutch Parliament, Donker formed a Commission of Enquiry. The first wave of retribution had swept the country. The traitors had been shot and the collaborators given prison sentences. There was every chance of the Enquiry being conducted in a calm atmosphere, especially as it was not a matter of bringing people to justice but of revealing the causes of the death of heroes.

Donker's first move was to ask the British Government for those responsible for the conduct of Special Operations Executive to give evidence before the Commission. The War Office replied that it was not desirable. Donker repeated his request, and again met with a refusal. He insisted, however, invoking human rights and calling upon all British subjects 'able to help the enquiry'. It was probably realised in London that Donker and the Dutch Government were prepared to take the matter before an International Court, for in April 1948, two Foreign Office officials were sent to The Hague to meet Donker. He had prepared some questions for them:

1. Had the chiefs of SOE deliberately sacrificed the lives of Dutch agents in the interests of other objectives?

2. Was it true that the agent H. G. Lauwers, when captured by the Germans, had sent coded messages to England which clearly showed that he was transmitting under control?

3. Had the British sent one or more agents to check on the SOE radio posts in Holland?

4. Would it be reasonable to suppose that some British officials might have been in the pay of the Germans? (Schreieder had insinuated this on several occasions during his interrogation by the Dutch.)

Donker did not believe in doing things by half! The two British officials rejected all these allegations as being without foundation. There had been no traitor at Baker Street. Not a single agent had been deliberately sacrificed. As for Lauwers's messages, there was no record of their having been received, but 'because of the great number of messages and the overworked cipher clerks, they might have escaped notice'.

The two officials returned to London. Donker and his Commission of Enquiry had made no headway. At the same time, the few survivors of the 'English Game' had been called to give evidence. But all they could say was, 'We know nothing, we are only the victims'. The Dutch newspapers were making accusations against Major Bingham, who had been responsible for training the Dutch agents.

In order to clear up the whole affair, Donker asked for the assistance of the Foreign Office and permission to pursue his enquiries in Britain. All this was granted. It was agreed that the British and the Dutch would collaborate in the common aim of throwing light on the murky business.

Donker and his colleagues went to London, and for several weeks they questioned those responsible for the conduct of SOE operations.

The officers whom Donker met were Major-General Sir Colin Gubbins (SOE), Mr Laming (SOE), Brigadier Mockler-Ferryman (SOE), Colonel Brook (SOE), Colonel Cordeaux (Intelligence Service), Mr Miller (SOE), Mr Seymour (Intelligence Service), Colonel Rabagliatti (Intelligence Service).

They revealed the workings of SOE and the apparatus of the Dutch Section to Donker and his colleagues. But the records had vanished! There had been a fire at the Baker Street offices in February 1946 – 'due to the negligence of an employee'. Most of the archives had been saved, but not, alas, those of the Dutch Section! The Dutch Parliamentary Commission was able to collect only verbal evidence. Lauwers's messages had all been burnt, Dourlein's message from Haaren had been burnt, a British Intelligence agent's report on the state of the Dutch Resistance in 1943 had been burnt. Donker and his colleagues questioned Major Bingham for hours, delving into his past, but in the end he was cleared of all accusations. Donker, intent on finding the truth, met with a blank wherever he turned. The 'English Game' had vanished into an abyss where History and Justice never tread.

Two years after the Dutch Commission had been set up, the Foreign Office issued a statement 'for Doctor L. A. Donker, Chairman of the Netherlands Parliamentary Commission of Enquiry'.

Its main points were as follows:

'During the last year enquiries have been received relating to the evidence put before the Netherlands tribunal concerning the conduct of clandestine operations in Holland and the German penetration of Resistance movements... Certain allegations have appeared in the Netherlands Press and elsewhere to the effect that the British military authorities, in so far as they were responsible for the conduct of these operations, had other ends in view than those which they declared to the Netherlands authorities. There is not a shred of truth in these allegations; in organising sabotage in the Netherlands, and in supporting the Netherlands Resistance Movement, the British authorities were guided by one consideration only—to attack the enemy in those areas where the Allied forces were not in contact with the German Army...

'The suggestion that the British authorities departed from the objectives which they had agreed with their Dutch colleagues and, in particular, the suggestion that the lives of Dutch patriots were deliberately sacrificed in the interests of other objectives, are both repugnant to His Majesty's Government and the British people and entirely lacking in foundation...

'... In March 1942, when the messages from the agent Lauwers began to arrive without the proper security checks, the Senior Netherlands Officer, then Colonel de Bruyne, was not in a position to check the text of the signals received and despatched.

'... Investigations were held at various periods after the original penetration had begun, but in each case a decision was taken to continue the operations. These decisions were reached after taking into consideration the personalities and character of the agents, and with the knowledge that the security checks had been proved in other cases to be inconclusive as a test. It was later realised that the decision to continue the operation was mistaken. . .

'The enquiry conducted at the time in Great Britain was necessarily incomplete, because no evidence on the German side was then available. But it is conclusively established that the original penetration was due solely to the operations of the German counter-intelligence, and that these produced a chain reaction owing to the system of reception committees which were jointly considered necessary owing to conditions in Holland, especially in view of the highly restricted dropping areas. . .

'The various and searching enquiries held by His Majesty's Government into the failure of Special Operations Executive operations in the Netherlands during 1942 and 1943, *leaving aside such errors of judgment as may have occurred in the course of their conduct* (my italics), have not revealed the slightest grounds for believing that there was treachery either on the British or on the Netherlands side.

'For reasons of elementary security the organisations in the field controlled respectively by SOE, whose function was to organise sabotage and resistance, and by the Intelligence Service, whose function was restricted to the acquisition of intelligence, were kept entirely separate. Hence it follows that there was no collaboration between the headquarters of these two organisations in the operational sphere and only such occasional collaboration in intelligence matters as was necessary to ensure that each received information of direct interest to itself. When the Intelligence Service received information that the SOE operations in Holland had been penetrated, SOE headquarters in London were immediately notified. Such information was not, however, received until May 1943.

'. . . When the original penetration began, Major Bingham was not in charge of the British side of the section and was not in a position to decide policy. He himself was opposed to the system of reception committees, and as soon as he took charge (in March 1943) insisted on doing away with it and adopting the more secure system of the 'blind drop'. Major Bingham was also responsible for ensuring that Dutch officers should be able to examine actual texts of telegrams where appropriate. . .'

This statement and the six thousand pages of the Commission's report did not satisfy the Dutch. Not only did the major questions remain unanswered, but fresh ones were raised. There was, for instance, that frightening admission: 'Investigations were held at various periods after the original penetration had begun, but in each case a decision was taken to continue the operations.' When were these investigations held, and by whom? If they were indeed carried out, it is hardly conceivable that the Intelligence officers responsible did not discover that some forty SOE agents were in prison and that a number of them had been turned. Even a second-rate Intelligence agent could have learned what had happened to Takonis, Baatsen, Lauwers and Jambroes.

Again, we read: 'It is conclusively established that the original penetration was due solely to the operations of the German counter-intelligence ...' Why the insinuation that at the beginning, but only at the beginning, it was the Germans who were entirely responsible for the 'English Game'? Did that mean that later they were helped? And if so, by whom? Was this meant to incriminate Lauwers, or to leave the door open in case a traitor was discovered later?

Then we read that the truth about the 'English Game' became known only in May 1943. That being so, why were the agents Brey, Mink and Punt despatched on 22 May? Did the British learn the truth in the last week of May? Or were Brey, Mink and Punt the agents with the mission of investigating the penetration? Or what?

There is also the tone of the statement – the offhand way in which it refers to 'errors of judgment as may have occurred in the course of operations'. The Dutch saw those errors as having caused the death of forty-eight patriots. On the scale of a world war, it was a small number. But for them, and for their pride, it was a tremendous number. The agents were not even mentioned in the statement, nor was Dourlein's escape from prison. No paragraph was included to honour the Dutchmen's sacrifice. In effect, the British statement was no more than a somewhat feeble justification of certain attitudes adopted by their secret services. The Dutch found it lacking in essentials.

The British finally put a stop to further investigation. They could do this quite legally through the Official Secrets Act (no British subject who has held an official position may reveal anything of secret operations, without permission, until forty years

have elapsed). The British authorities had already stretched
a point in allowing a foreign commission to search the SOE
archives (or rather, what was left of them after the fire).

That being said, the British can hardly be blamed for explaining away the errors of the SOE Dutch Section by the overloaded
radio communications, too much amateurism and the separation
of Intelligence services, in other words by lack of experience. As
for the charge of sacrificing agents' lives in the interests of other
objectives, it is difficult to see what could have been the aim. It is
possible that 'Plan Holland' was intended to divert attention from
the Dieppe raid. But then, why should it have been prolonged for
another fifteen months?

The suggestion that the British were hoping to learn some
German strategic secrets through the *England Spiel* channels is
equally improbable. Neither Giskes nor Schreieder was in the confidence of the German High Command. They were not even 'in
the know' concerning the plans of German Army HQ in Holland.
Besides, as soon as they controlled all the radio posts, the Germans would send only information that was false or of very minor
importance. It would not have been worth while for the British
to try to use the *England Spiel* from their end. They would have
been tying down a great number of experts for nothing.

There remains the theory (often put forward by the British
themselves) that, knowing the first agents were captured and
turned, the decision was made to continue the operation in order
to save their lives. In other words, the deepest cynicism gave way
to the gentlest feeling for human lives – in 1942, in the darkest
hours of the war! No, to pump fresh blood into an organism
known to be beyond resuscitation, that is nonsense. SOE was far
from being a charity!

Another theory has been advanced, independent of the findings of the Dutch Parliamentary Commission, by Major De Graaf,
who was a chief instructor with SOE between 1941 and 1944. He
was a friend of De Bruyne, Lieftinck and other Dutch secret service officers, and it is certain that he shares a number of secrets
with them.

His theory is as follows.

'In 1942 and 1943 a young man who was to achieve much
notoriety served as liaison officer between Baker Street and the
War Office. His name was Guy Burgess. He had been a convinced

(?) Communist since his Oxford days, was a homosexual and a man who could be bought. It is my belief that, through idealism or friendship, or simply for money, he made a traffic in the messages he conveyed to and from Baker Street. The Russians may well have been interested in destroying the British sabotage groups in Holland in order that the Communist groups could dominate the Dutch Resistance movement. Secondly, I repeat that Burgess, although an idealist, was fond of money. So it is possible that the Germans had bought him, purely and simply. Moreover, his morals laid him open to blackmail. The services of Guy Burgess could therefore be obtained for a very reasonable sum. But that is not all. In 1952, when Burgess and Maclean escaped to Russia, several Canadian and Australian papers printed a news agency report which accused Burgess of having sent fifty Dutch patriots to their death. I have not kept the cuttings from these papers, and I don't remember for certain the name of the agency which sent out the report.'

I have great respect for Major De Graaf, which is the only reason for my mentioning his theory. (He is, incidentally, the author of a fictionalized account of the *England Spiel*, entitled *Carneval der Desperados*, published in Amsterdam.) Unfortunately for his theory, Guy Burgess was employed at the Foreign Office in 1942 and 1943, and had little or no contact with SOE.

However, it would seem that there is a grain of truth in each of these theories. It seems obvious that the British received Lauwers's messages, as well as Dourlein's. But they could not reasonably conclude that *all* the SOE radio posts in Holland were controlled by the enemy. On the matter of the security checks, any specialist at that period would agree that it was a physical impossibility to note whether they were always included. With so many messages arriving from all over Europe, there just was not time. Giskes was quite right on this point – the British had put into operation a huge machine which soon became unmanageable (as they freely admitted). The dilapidated country house with a mere fifteen Signallers at work was hopelessly inadequate for dealing with all the flow of messages. A whole factory, properly equipped, and an army of technicians were needed. There was the fact, too, that operators in Occupied Europe worked under a very great strain and frequently omitted to include their security checks in their messages. Consequently, from August 1942, no attention was paid to the 'agreed mistakes'.

There can be no doubt that the British made some bad mistakes over the despatch of agents. The badly-forged identity papers, the obsolete currency, and the curious civilian uniform they were given, cannot be called 'errors of judgment'. It was downright negligence, from which not only Dutch agents suffered. Belgians and Norwegians were despatched on SOE mission with similar personal equipment, and it was a miracle that there were no other enemy operations of the 'North Pole' kind.

It had been said in some quarters that the reason for this negligence lies in the British attitude towards foreigners, the British way of looking down on 'aliens' as being 'without the law', but in wartime they had to be made use of, since they were allies. Then there are the usual sneers about *perfide Albion*. But all this is denied by the vast majority of foreigners who fought alongside the British throughout the war, by the Free French, the Free Danes, Belgians, Norwegians, in uniform or not – they all say that the British made no distinction of nationality in the fight against Nazism.

The most reasonable explanation seems to me that the British, far from having machiavellian intentions in this subversive warfare of their invention, really had no idea of the precautions necessary in Occupied Europe. (Even today, despite the progress made, one would be dismayed to see how inadequately prepared are some agents who are sent to foreign countries, especially from East Germany!) The Germans, on the other hand, were no amateurs. They had had plenty of experience during the subversive activities before the *Anschluss* and the annexation of Czechoslovakia!

I am quite aware that in time of war agents are sometimes deliberately sent by the one side into the arms of the enemy. Under torture, they tell what they know – but which, unbeknown to them, is false information. Mission accomplished. Yes, such things do happen.

The truth about Operation North Pole will not be found in this book. It went up in smoke in the Baker Street fire. I have set down the story of the Dutch Section of SOE. It was never my intention to sit in judgment. Besides, who would have the right to judge SOE?

Except in Holland, this organisation for subversive warfare did wonders. In France, the Ratier aircraft works at Toulouse and the Creusot factories were blown up several times by SOE agents. Sabotage groups repeatedly disrupted rail communications, destroyed dams and electricity transformers. In Denmark, SOE brought naval construction to a halt on several occasions, while in Norway the heavy water plant at Rjukan was blown up.

On the whole, Churchill's orders had been carried out. A few fires had been lit in Occupied Europe.

It was at Bildhoven, not far from Utrecht, that I met Hubertus Gerardus Lauwers. Neither Giskes nor Fate had wished him to die. He was sent to a German concentration camp some time after the rest of his comrades, being hustled into the last waggon of the last convoy to Germany. And in the spring of 1945 this traitor in name only was snatched from death's door by the Allies.

On his return to Holland he was reviled and threatened with arrest, so he sought British aid in clearing his name. He had heart trouble and was suffering from tuberculosis. Nevertheless, he went to London. There, not only was no explanation given him, but he was accused of treason. He was handed over to the Dutch. Lauwers appealed for help, and was on the point of being arrested when Major De Graaf turned up and gave evidence before the Commission of Enquiry. 'Lauwers is innocent,' he proclaimed. 'He did indeed warn London. I saw the messages.'

Lauwers was set free, but he was ill at ease in his freedom, as if wearing clothes much too large for him. He studied to be a dentist, and he married Teller's widow. The years went by, and he became an excellent dentist, even lecturing on stomatology at Utrecht University. But the gloomy thoughts did not leave him. Dark questions remained stuck in his mind. They will always be with him, for no one will ever supply the answers. He has been rehabilitated, certainly, but the findings of judges do not necessarily carry weight among the neighbours. People avoid him. At best, he is nodded to, though rarely with a smile. The Dutch have turned the page. They have not yet admitted that he is innocent. Fortunately, he still has a few friends.

Ten years ago, he made an application for the Willems Order, which carries a very fine medal. His application met with refusal. I dedicate this book to Hubertus Gerardus Lauwers.

Index